W9-DHR-852

Circus Heroes and Heroines

by
Rhina Kirk

HAMMOND®
INCORPORATED

Acknowledgments

The author wishes to thank the many kind people who were helpful in providing research materials for this book, including members of the staffs of The Historical Association of Pennsylvania, Free Library of Philadelphia, Lower Merion Library Association, Haverford Township Free Library, Texas History and Genealogy Department of the Dallas Public Library and the Hertzberg Circus Collection of the San Antonio Public Library.

A special debt must be acknowledged to all of those who provided information based on their expertise with the circus:

John Hurdle: Ringling Museum of the Circus
Robert L. Parkinson: Circus World Museum
Frank Taylor, Dr. Bradley J. Kwenski: Circus Hall of Fame
Kenneth B. Holmes and staff: Barnum Museum
James Dunwoody: Circus Fans Association
Ford "Happy" Wand, Bill Bailey: Clowns of America
Harry T. Hunt: Hunt Brothers Circus
Wolcott Fenner, Jack Ryan: Ringling Bros. and Barnum & Bailey Combined Shows, Inc.
Art Concello, Antoinette Concello, Merle Evans, Emmett Kelly, Karl Wallenda, May Wirth and many other performers.

Special gratitude to:

Bernard A. Kirshbaum, Donna, Randa and Paul, Margaret Cooke, Donald E. Cooke, Ernest Dupuy and Sally Sylk for help and encouragement with the manuscript.

Acknowledgement is also made to Ringling Bros. and Barnum & Bailey Combined Shows, Inc., for permission to reproduce certain circus posters which are copyright material owned by them. Ringling Bros. and Barnum & Bailey™, The Greatest Show on Earth ™ are trademarks of Ringling Bros. and Barnum & Bailey Combined Shows, Inc.

Title Page illustrations: Acrobats poster, Circus World Museum, Baraboo, Wisconsin; Wallenda high-wire act, U.P.I. photo.

Library of Congress Cataloging in Publication Data
Kirk, Rhina.
    Circus heroes and heroines.
    SUMMARY: Brief profiles of famous circus personalities such as P. T. Barnum, Tom Thumb, Clyde Beatty, and Annie Oakley plus a short history of the origins of the circus.
    Bibliography: p.91
    1. Circus — Biography — Juvenile literature.
(1. Circus-Biography)   I. Title.
GVI811.A1K5   791.3'092'2   74-189632
ISBN 0-8437-3879-0
ISBN 0-8437-3979-7 (lib. bdg.)

Contents

1
Introduction

Beginnings and Early Showmen

The breathtaking acrobatic and wild animal acts of the modern circus can be traced at least as far back as 2400 B.C.! A wall painting excavated by archaeologists on the island of Crete depicts athletic youths leaping over charging bulls. This feat was performed in an arena before crowds who sat on raised seats. Murals painted centuries later in Egypt show acrobats, jugglers, and tumblers performing their routines. The Greeks also had acrobats and tumblers who leaped and danced over swords.

However, the circus of ancient times was brought to its greatest heights of glory and depravity under the Romans. In fact, our word "circus" is taken from the Roman Circus Maximus, a huge, roofless structure which was U-shaped, 625 yards long, with tiered sides capable of holding several hundred thousand curious, thrill-seeking spectators at one time. This large public arena was used primarily for chariot racing, but on many occasions animals and men were slain in great numbers to please the bloodthirsty cravings of emperors and the mobs who assembled to watch these events. Acrobats also put on tumbling acts before these audiences, but chariot racing was by far the most popular contest. The daring charioteers driving teams of two or four horses vied with each other in these furious races. Although admission to the Circus Maximus was free, nearby merchants did a thriving business selling pastries, wine and souvenirs; forerunners of the present-day "candy butchers."

During the eightieth year of the Christian Era, the Roman General Titus dedicated the Colosseum. Though somewhat smaller than the Circus Maximus, the elliptical form of this amphitheater gave the people a clearer view of the performances. These often consisted of Christian prisoners battling unarmed against enraged lions, tigers and other wild beasts. Gladiators also fought each other to the death. After these brutal displays the stadium was often sprayed with perfume and sand was spread over the blood on the floor.

As the great Roman Empire began to totter, these gory spectacles diminished. Maccus, one of the earliest recorded clowns, decried the lack of humor in the Colosseum exhibitions during this decline. Those who followed the profession of Maccus subsequently helped to develop the role of court jester and the itinerant troupes of entertainers, including jugglers, rope dancers, tumblers and minstrels. During the Dark Ages of medieval Europe and for many years afterward, groups of adventurous performers and instrumentalists wandered from town to town where they gratefully accepted the meager coins dropped into the hat which they passed around. The arena-type circus program did not reappear for over a thousand years.

At English fairs of the seventeenth and eighteenth centuries, acrobats, fortune tellers and dancing gypsies entertained the townspeople, while a carnival-like atmosphere was created by sideshows and menageries that were close by. But the circus as we know it

MUSEUM OF THE CITY OF NEW YORK

was not introduced until 1770 by a young cavalry sergeant, Philip Astley (1742-1814). Formerly a member of the British Light Dragoons and skilled in horsemanship, Astley is considered to be the father of the modern circus. It was he who planned and designed the first "ring" and gave to the world the circus format which is still used today.

Astley, the handsome son of a British cabinetmaker, discovered that centrifugal force could keep a man standing on a horse while galloping around in a circle. He embellished this stunt by riding around the ring with one foot on the saddle and one foot on the horse's head while fearlessly waving a broadsword. In addition to his own remarkable agility, he supplemented the show with a clown act, "Billie Button, or the Tailor's Ride to Brentwood," which became famous at that time, as well as with a juggler, tightrope walker, dancing dogs and musicians. One such performance was called "The Egyptian Pyramid, An Amusing Performance of Men Piled Upon Men." Some features of those early shows are still used in circuses today. Although Astley's program included various supporting acts, it was his daring exhibitions on horseback which dominated the show. In those early days he encountered many personal hardships; fires repeatedly destroyed the buildings where he performed.

When Astley took his company to France, he encountered a group of circus performers, the Franconi family. Astley demonstrated his style of horsemanship which they incorporated into their own show. The Franconi family later perfected the proportions of the ring and established the first open-air hippodrome in France. The "spec" or spectacular which opens most present-day circus shows is also attributed to the Franconi family.

In 1785 the first native American performer, Thomas Pool, began to demonstrate extraordinary trick riding abilities at his Philadelphia Riding School. The first complete circus presentation, however, was put together by an English equestrian who had come to the United States in 1793. John Bill Ricketts (176?-1799) presented a varied program consisting not only of unusual stunts on horseback, but rope walkers, tumblers, and a British clown, Tom Sully, who delighted audiences with his famous song, "Four and Twenty Perriwigs." There were also pantomime and other forms of dramatic entertainment, but the daring men on horseback galloping around the ring continued to be the main attraction of these shows.

President George Washington, who shared an appreciation of horses, made it a special point to attend these performances in Philadelphia in 1793. He delighted in watching Ricketts leap from his horse, Cornplanter, through a hoop suspended twelve feet in the air, alighting again on the saddle of the trotting horse. As a result of his acceptance by President Washington, Ricketts' circus was assured of success, and he was able to open an amphitheater in New York in addition to the one in Philadelphia. Both of these buildings were to suffer the same fate that befell Astley's ventures; they also burned to the ground. Bankrupt and discouraged he left for England in 1799, but the ship that he sailed on was lost at sea.

An American shipmaster from Salem, Captain Jacob Crowninshield, made an original contribution to American circus history in 1796 by bringing the first elephant to this country from Bengal, which he advertised as being "upwards of 8 feet and weighing more than 5,700 pounds." In 1815 another elephant became familiar to curious townspeople in Somers, New York, and surrounding areas. Hachaliah Bailey purchased Old Bet for $1000, and the exhibition of this huge elephant was so successful that the owner added more animals to his traveling exhibit.

9

John Bill Ricketts
staged the first complete circus
performances in America.

PRINCETON UNIVERSITY LIBRARY, THEATRE COLLECTION

Other aspiring showmen saw the potential of financial reward in these menageries and exhibited their animals in any convenient yard or field. One of these entrepreneurs was "General" Rufus Welch (1801-1856), who knew that pleasing the public with exotic creatures would make him rich. He traveled to Africa and brought back numerous wild animals which he took on tour.

The number of touring menagerie exhibitors was now increasing, and in 1835 one such group formed the Zoological Institute in New York City which not only housed and leased animals but organized and managed early circus operations. Some of the original investors in this corporation went on to form a separate group called the Flatfoots, earning this appellation by stating firmly when trying to accomplish some business maneuver, "I put my foot down flat!" The Flatfoots were a strong and brash syndicate which dominated the field of menageries and circus companies for many years.

It must be recalled that at this time the circus shows were considered by the general population to be frivolous and sinful— in the same class as the theater — and most people preferred to visit the menageries. The eventual marriage of these two forms of entertainment, the circus-menagerie, took place in the 1830's.

To announce the arrival and promote the small traveling wagon shows, an "advance man" and a clown often were sent out a few days earlier to those towns earmarked for stops. The advance man would post bills in places that were sure to catch the attention of the townsfolk and country people. These small troupes at first traveled in conestoga-type covered wagons and subsequently in regular horse-drawn wagons, moving from town to town mostly by night over bumpy country roads. They were often the victims of bad weather, and as a result their shows came to be known as "mud shows," since the wagon wheels frequently bogged down and they were stalled in the mud. The reception given to these rolling wagon shows was sometimes friendly, but more often hostile, as circuses were still not acceptable entertainment.

A few permanent buildings for shows were built in the larger cities along the eastern coast of the United States. In some of these, animal trainers began to risk their lives daringly for the approval of those who came to see them. One who was well known at that time was Isaac Van Amburgh (1801-1865), who astonished audiences in a New York theater by being the first man to put his head inside a lion's mouth. He was also the first to put a lion and a lamb together in one cage. Later a child was added to prove that all three could stay peaceably in one enclosure. Van Amburgh became successful enough to start his own show, which included Hannibal, the largest elephant exhibited up to that time in the United States. His company also featured a gigantic circus wagon which led a parade of colorful cages down the streets of New York City in the 1830's. The spectacular and ornate wagons and parades became an important tradition of the American circus only to disappear less than a century later. Although Van Amburgh died in 1865, his name was used in the title of circus companies for many years afterward.

There were many other showmen who owned companies in which they also performed. Joseph A. Rowe successfully played to Gold Rush audiences in California in the 1840's, only to fail financially after the boom was over. Levi J. North, billed as the "North Star," was a good-looking horseback rider who startled audiences with his daring somersault stunts on a swiftly moving horse. The names of two brothers were synonymous with the early expansion of the American circus: Nathan A. Howes (1796-1878) and Seth B. Howes (1815-1901). Nathan Howes and his early partner Aaron Turner were the first men in America to organize a full show under a round-top canvas — the first tented circus. A troupe under the ownership of the younger brother, Seth Howes, traveled to London and performed successfully there under the title, Seth B. Howes Great European and Great London Circuses. This company was a highly respected name in circus history both here and abroad for many years.

In 1856 another team of circus proprietors, Spalding and Rogers, began to utilize the vast possibilities of water travel by means of a showboat which they named the *Floating Palace*. Towed by steam-driven paddle boat, the *Palace* went up and down the Mississippi River, putting on shows at many river towns until the 1860's, when the Civil War intervened. The Dan Rice Circus was another which plied the great Mississippi on a showboat.

A landmark in circus history which drastically changed the pattern and scope of companies reaching distant parts of the country was the advent of rail travel. However, there still remained a number of small regional companies which traveled by horse-drawn wagons to remote areas.

Along this arduous road from the mud shows to the spangled world of the modern circus, courageous men and women surmounted difficulties unparalleled in any other form of entertainment. A kaleidoscope of heroic personalities, from a political jester of the 1800's to a family who, despite numerous tragedies, continues to perform on the high wire up to this day, will be viewed in the following chapters.

11

2
Dan Rice

Although many clowns have been able to establish immediate rapport with their audiences, none have had the great personal magnetism that Dan Rice exerted on his viewers in the mid-nineteenth century. Dan Rice was an extraordinary clown, a bright and talented comic, highly sensitive to the social and political climate of his time, whose original style gained him great popularity. However, his career and personality were highly erratic, marked by sundry problems including bankruptcy, alcoholism and a fickle public that propelled him to fame, but just as readily cast him off.

Dan Rice was the first American who was both an equestrian and a clown. He could verbally juggle Shakespearean quotes and political quips and put on remarkable exhibitions of bareback riding — all in one performance! This bizarre circus jester with dark, piercing eyes and stentorian voice, considered by circus buffs to be one of the greatest clowns of all time — also wanted to be President of the United States.

Daniel McLaren, Jr., was born in New York City on January 23, 1823. His mother was the daughter of a Methodist minister; his father a law student who later became a groceryman. During the boy's early years his mother remarried, this time to a dairyman who was greatly interested in horses. This abiding love for horses was passed on to young Daniel who became a jockey at age ten. About this time his maternal grandfather suggested changing his name to Dan Rice — a name which he used throughout the remainder of his tempestuous and, at times, brilliant career. His services were much sought after, but his career as a jockey ended at age seventeen when he became too heavy for the saddle. At that time (1840), Dan Rice went to Pittsburgh and, because of his fondness for horses, secured a job as a general helper in a livery stable.

One of the early traveling circuses, the Nichols Circus, was performing close to where Dan worked, and he quickly made friends among the circus people. He learned many tricks from the equestrian and the strong man who appeared in the show. He learned to pitch cannon balls from his shoulder and earned the name Young Hercules from the other troupers. His enthusiasm for this exciting life became progressively greater, but he continued to work as a hired hand at the stable. While traveling on a boat to transport some horses for his employer, young Dan Rice met the renowned Senator Henry Clay. Dan entertained the senator and others on board by dancing some jigs and singing a tune, which he had recently composed, called "Hard Times." The impromptu performance was warmly received by Senator Clay who awarded him another nickname, Yankee Dan.

Dan returned to the Nichols Circus in Pittsburgh but learned that in his absence it had been sold. The new owner was a scholarly looking former druggist from Albany, N.Y., "Dr." Gilbert B. Spalding (1811-1880), who ironically became both a friend and the nemesis of Dan Rice for several decades. Dr. Spalding quickly recognized the enormous talents of the young man and persuaded him to join the show.

The strength and versatility of Dan Rice were almost boundless. He was the strong man and circus jester. Dan also developed a routine with an educated pig whom he called Lord Byron. The animal would respond to questions asked of him by scratching his foot on the ground for the correct answer. This trick was based on Dan Rice's observation that pigs had an extremely keen ability to hear. By clicking his fingernails, Dan was able to get the pig to paw the ground for the appropriate number of times. The pig was also trained to select an American flag from

Dan Rice, America's first great clown,
in top hat and chin whiskers
inspired Uncle Sam cartoon figure.

a box and wave it before an amazed audience. Some townspeople, however, could not accept this mysterious animal act, believing it to be a phenomenon caused by "evil spirits" or witchcraft. And in the churches, which always had opposed the circus, sermons were preached on its wickedness.

Dan Rice gave to Dr. Spalding's circus all of his enormous talents and energies, but he felt that he could receive more money and expand his abilities by working for someone else. He joined the Nathan A. Howes Circus in 1845, but the association did not last long. For another brief period he was with the Rufus Welch Company. Dan was becoming more independent as a performer all the time. In 1848 he decided to strike out on his own and opened "Dan Rice's Great Circus."

In those days of the one-ring circus, the clown was the dominant feature. Dan danced and sang songs of a topical nature, lampooning current events and people. "Root Hog or Die" was a popular ditty which he composed and which the people asked for over and over again. Another tune which he composed, "Red, White and Blue," was also frequently sung. He performed this number with his newly acquired wife, Margaret Ann Curran, who also appeared in a colorful costume in the show. He bantered with the ringmaster and a delighted audience, often using appropriate quotations from Shakespeare. In addition to the act with his pig Lord Byron, he added a rope-walking elephant, named Lalla Rookh, for the heroine of a Persian poem.

Even in his appearance Dan Rice was original. He grew chin whiskers which jutted forward. His face was memorable for its piercing eyes which seemed to penetrate you when looking at him, though he was actually a very gentle man. A red and white striped costume and a top hat perched on his head became his trademark, which Thomas Nast, the famous illustrator for *Harper's Weekly*, caricatured into the symbol for Uncle Sam.

In the latter part of 1848, Dan Rice abandoned wagons as a means of circus travel in favor of a steamboat, *The Allegheny Mail*. Animals and equipment were loaded onto the riverboat and as its paddle wheels

churned, it journeyed down the Mississippi River to New Orleans, stopping at river towns along the way to put on shows. At the Mississippi delta, the paddle boat reversed its course and headed back to St. Paul, Minnesota.

In the following year, the first of a series of misfortunes struck the ambitious showman. He developed yellow fever, which forced him to cancel the circus boat tour that year. While recovering in a New Orleans hospital, he met General Zachary Taylor, who was visiting there. This meeting marked the beginning of a long and lasting friendship which continued for many years. When Dan Rice was well enough to return to work, he made campaign speeches for Taylor, the presidential aspirant, before each regular performance. Taylor did become president, and it was thought that Dan's active campaigning from the circus ring was helpful in the election. In gratitude President Taylor named Dan Rice an aide with the title of colonel. The career of Colonel Dan Rice flourished as a result of presidential publicity, but he also became more egotistical with the new adulation. His moods changed as frequently as a weathervane.

Dr. Spalding again appeared on the scene. Well aware of the comic's drawing powers at the crest of success, he asked Dan to join another circus he was forming. Dan accepted, but the association was short-lived and soon terminated. Other alliances were similarly formed and disregarded; contracts were torn and thrown into the air like confetti. The behavior pattern of this highly temperamental artist became well-known. The feud between Spalding and Rice flared, especially whenever the rival companies appeared near one another. Inflammatory statements allegedly made by Rice about Spalding and his partner (Spalding's brother-in-law) resulted in Dan Rice's arrest for slander in 1850. The brief time spent in jail, however, did not still his talents, for it was here that Dan composed "Blue Eagle Jail," a song which attired him in the cloak of martyrdom by its sad tale of wrongful imprisonment. When he was released from the prison near Rochester, N.Y., Dan was welcomed back as a hero.

With renewed zeal, he organized a show which was legendary in its time — Dan Rice's One-Horse-Show. It featured his famous horse, Excelsior, which he trained to walk down portable stairs one step at a time. One of the acts of this show which is still used in some form in the modern circus is called the Pete Jenkins act. If you have ever watched a baggy trousered bumpkin of a clown try to get on a horse, stumble several times, fall off and try again, shedding his outer garments to reveal a magnificent costume, then ride off again in a blaze of splendor, you have seen the "Pete Jenkins from Mud Corners" sequence created over a century ago by this ingenious clown. The One-Horse-Show, with its many acts, proved so successful a venture when it ran as a summer show on the waterways that Dan opened an amphitheater in New Orleans for his winter performances. In his new quarters he added a larger menagerie and a museum. The show now included Mrs. Dan Rice as a star equestrienne, additional clowns, tightrope walkers, rope dancers and pole balancers as well as Lalla Rookh, the performing elephant.

Though most of Dan's songs and witty remarks were well received by the general public there were some critical newspaper men (especially Horace Greeley) who could not accept his lively brand of repartee. They considered him "unlearned" and a "language destroyer." But even his foes had to admit that his generosity and charity were exemplary. In the mid-1850's he often played for orphanages and delighted young audiences by giving special afternoon performances for them, a thing unheard of at that time. The critics persisted in their malevolent attacks against the "tanbark jester." Spurred on by their insistent opposition, Dan fought against their spiteful vendetta, maintaining even more outspoken dialogues with his audiences. He also strengthened those parts of the program in which he did not personally appear by adding more singers, dancers and other performers—more than any other one-ring show!

On the road, audiences packed Rice's performances to overflowing in the late 1850's and early 1860's. But the melancholic sounds of war drums were beginning to be heard in the land. Dan's problems were only starting. Performances were interrupted constantly by those who opposed his Republican views. Name calling and garbage hurling were common occurrences. Dan was often much too outspoken in his views. At the same time the sympathetic and sensitive entertainer offered his help and talents, frequently giving benefit performances for soldiers and war widows. At this time he was forced to play in buildings only in the largest cities. President Lincoln, though his heart was full of anguish over the hostilities, managed to find time to visit the circus when it appeared in a Washington theater, and legend has it that he visited Dan Rice after the show. However, during the following months, the war-troubled people did not attend the circus with any regularity. Dan Rice lost his company, and subsequently his wife left him. Within the space of two years, Dan Rice remarried.

In 1862, Dr. Spalding again tried to lure his former archenemy and sometime friend, Dan Rice, back into a partnership. He reasoned that, with his tent improvements and the magic of the Dan Rice banner, they could enjoy new vistas of success together. He made Dan Rice the startling offer of a

Theater barges like the *Floating Palace* were an innovation used by major circuses before the Civil War.

$1,000 weekly salary if he would join him, but Dan refused. He chose to continue on his own.

After the war was over Dan Rice organized another circus enterprise. With his characteristic seesaw luck, his purse was promptly filled as a result of this new undertaking. During a visit to his second wife's hometown Dan Rice directed that a monument be erected to honor the fallen war heroes at a cost of thousands of dollars. Dan had previously experienced dramatic swings of the financial pendulum, alternating between wealth and poverty. He then made an unwise business association with Adam Forepaugh's Menageries which caused him great financial loss.

By 1866 Dan was convinced that the world of entertainment was not his forté any longer. He was more intrigued by politics and began to make a number of speeches in Pennsylvania, thereby announcing his intensions of running for Congress from the Keystone state. In 1868 he was nominated by a soldiers' delegation which introduced a motion that Dan Rice be endorsed as a candidate for president! This again provoked an outcry from critics who advised him to stick to horses and not meddle with such noble matters as the presidency. Undaunted, Dan continued campaigning. Dan Rice for President clubs were formed. Tradesmen affixed signs on their windows which read "Rice for Pudding and President." However, the energy Dan devoted to his campaigning only weakened his image and popularity among those who had enjoyed his antics under the canvas top.

Once again Dr. Spalding appeared in Dan Rice's life. During the time that Dan was busy with his political ambitions, Spalding had devised an elegantly appointed portable wooden amphitheater complete with canvas top, which he called the *Paris Pavilion*. This could be set up on land or on a river barge pulled by a tugboat — a versatile and novel arrangement not previously attempted. After his brush with politics Dan returned to show business. Dreaming of the joys of owning this dazzling circus house, he purchased the *Paris Pavilion* from Spalding by borrowing heavily. His hopes were overoptimistic; the enormous expenses for this investment were far beyond his reach. Repeated disappointments, coupled with the general economic depression of the country, turned the once-vigorous and gentle man into an irritable and irresponsible person. He tried to drown his sorrows in alcohol and frequently recited his multitudinous problems to those who would listen.

Eventually, with great personal courage, he overcame his troubles by becoming a Temperance lecturer, giving speeches whenever and wherever he could find an audience. When he felt he had sufficient self-control he sought to reenter the circus business in California. But the public who once lined up at the box offices was no longer interested in the great clown and showman. The town he had given $35,000 to erect a Civil War monument refused to lend him even a token sum. By 1887 he laid aside his clown mantle and officially retired. This extremely individualistic, humane, and often pompous man lived a life filled with many victories and defeats. He gained a national reputation as an entertainer and through his colorful style of living. Dan Rice made his final exit in Long Branch, N. J., where he died of Bright's disease on February 22, 1900, at the age of seventy-seven.

3
P.T. Barnum

The Phenomenal Showman

In the spring of the year 1820, a young and innocent boy was shown five acres of land called Ivy Island by his grandfather who loved to play practical jokes. The boy had been given the land as a christening gift and had looked forward with much anticipation during his boyhood to seeing his precious legacy at last. Hope gave way to disillusionment as the youth realized that Ivy Island was just swampland.

Such deception practiced on a delicate ego might have shattered the dreams of anyone else of a similar age, but not *this* young man. The incident taught him an important lesson — always know when you are being fooled. The youthful owner of the worthless land was to become the greatest showman who ever lived and, like his grandfather before him, a prankster without malice.

Phineas Taylor Barnum was born in Bethel, Connecticut, on July 5, 1810, the first of five children born to Mr. and Mrs. Philo Barnum. Like many youngsters of that time he had to help support the expanding family. He worked at first on his father's farm and later as a clerk in a general store. Of necessity he had to forego many of his classes at the country school, finishing only six grades.

When Taylor, as he was called, was fifteen years old, his father died. The youth, who later became a millionaire several times over, was then so poor that he borrowed money for shoes to wear at his father's funeral.

It was while working as a clerk that young Barnum succeeded in his first business venture. A traveling peddler, pushing a cart loaded with green glass bottles which he wanted to get rid of, stopped by the general store when the owners were out. The youthful employee told the peddler that he would take the entire cartload. When the proprietors returned they were aghast at the sight of the seemingly valueless merchandise. Whereupon Taylor explained that he could dispose of the bottles in no time at all as prizes in a lottery, an idea popular at that time. Additional prizes were old tin cups, plates and other junk that had been piling up in the back of the store. The lottery succeeded and the experience proved valuable to Barnum.

After a few other odd jobs Barnum became restless. He wanted to have his own business instead of working for others. In 1828, just before his eighteenth birthday, he bought a small retail grocery. Though it was primarily a food store, young Barnum also made it a headquarters for a lottery agency. The two businesses prospered well until 1834, when the state of Connecticut made lotteries illegal. Barnum sold the business and moved to New York City where he settled with his wife and their small daughter. Mrs. Barnum was the former Charity Hallett, a seamstress from Bethel, whom he had married when he was nineteen.

BARNUM MUSEUM,
BRIDGEPORT, CONNECTICUT

17

MUSEUM OF THE CITY OF NEW YORK

Barnum's American Museum
on lower Broadway in
New York City.

Barnum bought another grocery store while Charity added to the family income by opening a boardinghouse. In July of 1835 a neighbor came into Barnum's store and told him of a remarkable elderly black woman by the name of Joice Heth, who had been George Washington's nursemaid and was reputedly one hundred and sixty-one years old! The neighbor, Coley Bartram, stated that there were legal documents to support these claims and that the woman, though partially paralyzed, was still alert and still able to sing hymns. Young Barnum, a strapping six-foot-two-inch man then in his mid-twenties and always ready for new adventures, traveled down to Philadelphia to see the ancient Negress.

Barnum was so impressed by the woman that upon his return to New York he sold his business, borrowed an additional $500.00 and "bought" Joice Heth. He made the arrangements for her to be brought to New York where he exhibited her adjacent to Niblo's Garden, a popular cabaret. She was placed on a high table in a special exhibition room where, in her ancient raiment, she was displayed. People came from miles around, lining up outside in eager anticipation of seeing this human curiosity. The price which Barnum had to pay in Philadelphia for his find was almost doubly repaid in a very short while.

After the death of Joice Heth a few months later, her true age was disclosed. The doctor who performed the autopsy shocked the young entrepreneur by revealing that she was no more than eighty, at best. It is uncertain whether or not Barnum actually knew this at the time he exhibited Joice Heth, but, in an autobiography which was published later, Barnum said that he was convinced of the authenticity of her age because of her documents. However, one thing is certain — Barnum became convinced that the public liked to be fooled and that they knew the exaggerated claims might not be true. This belief may be linked to the often repeated, but not substantiated, phrase attributed to Barnum, that there's a sucker born every minute.

After this successful but brief introduction to show business, Barnum became fascinated by the idea of promoting curiosities. But first he needed more experience in the circus field, and in 1836 he secured a job as a ticket collector in Aaron Turner's traveling circus show. Barnum also made a few unsuccessful attempts to assemble a show of his own. Interestingly enough, the association with the Aaron Turner group was to be Barnum's only close contact with a true circus for the next thirty-five years!

In the early 1840's Barnum learned that John Scudder's American Museum in New York City was for sale. Although benefiting from a very good location in the heart of the rapidly growing city, the museum had become run-down after Scudder's death. It exhibited such oddities as a mechanical device run by a dog, stuffed animals, dioramas, waxworks and other curios. Barnum, with his uncanny foresight, believed that he could enliven it with fresher, more exciting collections and make it a profitable business. The only problem was lack of money. Remembering his childhood experience he told the proprietors of the museum that he owned a very valuable property called Ivy Island in Connecticut. Barnum's persuasive

Depiction of Feejee Mermaid,
a hoax promoted by Barnum,
from a broadside for his museum.

powers sufficiently impressed those involved so that he was able to lease the building in 1841 with no capital. Almost immediately he set about changing the museum. The magic touch of the neophyte showman became evident everywhere. Exhibits were either altered or completely discarded. Live shows with knife throwers, magicians and ventriloquists were added. Barnum sought to give the visitors as great a variety as possible for their twenty-five-cent admission.

By 1847 Barnum's American Museum became a dazzling showplace, surrounded by an aura that America had never known before. In his eagerness to make the place constantly more spectacular, Barnum began collecting as many strange creatures, bizarre objects and different types of wild beasts as he could to add to those already in the museum. He added Punch and Judy and other puppet shows. He promoted a working model of Niagara Falls as "the Great Model of Niagara Falls" even though the cataract was only eighteen inches high.

To further advertise the attractions of his show, brightly colored posters were displayed on the outside of his museum, giving the passersby on Broadway some idea of the current exhibits inside. Barnum also had a keen sense of humor. He hired a group of musicians who played poorly and installed them on a balcony above the museum entrance. When asked why he hired such inadequate musicians, Barnum replied that if they played badly enough the people would want to go inside to escape their raspy sounds!

The museum prospered with one success following another. Barnum's debts were soon paid off and a handsome profit was beginning to appear on the books. The fertile mind of the showman was always buzzing with some dramatic way to promote the museum and to lure customers.

The crowds coming to visit Barnum's American Museum were so tremendous that it became difficult at times to cope with them. On one particular St. Patrick's day hordes of people came, visited the exhibition halls, ate their lunches, then crowded the rooms to gape at the exhibits all over again. Barnum wanted them to move along so that others waiting outside could get in. He himself solved the problem by having signs made which read, "To the Egress." People thought that it was pointing to another exotic animal and obediently followed the signs which led to a doorway and the street.

One of the most fantastic bits of trickery that Barnum ever perpetrated was that of the "Feejee Mermaid." He ordered posters and handbills printed which extolled the wonders of this half-woman, half-fish specimen. Though the original idea was not conceived by Barnum himself, the idea of exploiting it was developed by the able mind of the showman. Barnum had purchased this oddity from a Boston museum which had obtained it from some Japanese fishermen in the Fiji Islands. The Feejee Mermaid creature was actually a dried monkey's head and torso meticulously sewn and glued to the lower half of a salmon-like fish. The job was so artistically done that it was very difficult to see where the two parts were joined. The showman was well aware of the fraud but nevertheless exhibited it to the horror and fascination of the spectators.

Undoubtedly Phineas Taylor Barnum's most successful attraction was the engaging twenty-five-inch midget, General Tom Thumb. Barnum's promotion of Tom Thumb and the famous elephant, Jumbo, are described in subsequent chapters.

Barnum's American Museum was one of the foremost landmarks in New York City during the middle of the nineteenth century. The continuing parade of unusual curiosities exhibited in that era justified this designation.

Besides the celebrated Tom Thumb, there were Anna Swan, the pleasant-looking giantess from Nova Scotia who was seven feet eleven inches tall and weighed four hundred and thirteen pounds and Madame Clofullia, the bearded lady who was the target of a law suit which threw doubts upon her sex, a publicity stunt instigated by the Great Hoaxer himself!

But Barnum almost out-Barnumed himself when he presented to the awestruck visitors a most unexpected attraction — the Siamese twins, Chang and Eng. Curiously enough they were not Siamese but born to Chinese parents in Siam. These two brothers were joined together by a thick skin-covered ligament at their lower chests. Today two people joined abnormally are still referred to as Siamese twins.

Barnum brought Chang and Eng to his museum after they had been exhibited for a number of years in other showplaces around the world. Barnum didn't care for them much—perhaps because he did not personally discover them and they had already enjoyed popularity elsewhere. The twins were not exactly in harmony with the showman either. They felt he was stingy and an exploiter. They also disliked each other and often quarreled. They were completely opposite in temperament — what one liked the other disliked. Eng was rather docile and a tee-totaler while Chang was hostile and drank heavily. The only things they had in common were hunting, fishing and a great desire to be severed from each other. Although several surgeons were consulted, none could promise a successful operation.

At the age of forty-two after having made a great deal of money, the twins retired to a North Carolina plantation. They married daughters of an Irish farmer and resolved the problem of housing by devising an equitable arrangement. Chang and Eng lived for part of the week with Chang's wife in one of the two houses which they had built. Then the Siamese twins spent the rest of the week with Eng's wife in the second house nearby. Twenty-one children were born of this strange union. The men both died on the same day in 1874.

The steady stream of successes in his bizarre business of human oddities filled the showman's pockets. But P. T. Barnum was aching for something beyond this— something more artistic and cultural to absorb his time and energies. Priding himself on his appreciation of the finer things in life, he wanted to try his hand at being an impresario.

Barnum was familiar with the record-breaking response Europeans had given the Swedish Nightingale, Jenny Lind. To be able

BARNUM MUSEUM,
BRIDGEPORT, CONNECTICUT

to import this illustrious singer would certainly give Barnum the prestige he sought at that time. He sent an agent to Europe to try to convince her to come to America. At first the temperamental diva was reluctant to perform under the sponsorship of a "showman," but she was persuaded that he was a responsible individual and that she should try her luck in America.

Barnum realized that his star was relatively unknown in the United States, and he promptly started an enormous campaign to publicize Jenny Lind and familiarize Americans with her name and talent even before she reached these shores. Jenny Lind arrived in August 1850 and made her debut at Castle Garden in New York on September 11. The critics' response after the concert, which had included a standing ovation, was overwhelming. There were a few dissident remarks from some critics but most were enchanted. New Yorkers paid over $87,000 for her first six concerts. Soon songs were dedicated to her while articles of clothing and novelties bore her name.

After the success in New York a personal appearance tour of the eastern cities and Cuba began. Soon the strain of travel, coupled with her own mercurial temperament, which was depressed one moment and joyous the next, proved too much. Despite the success of the tour, friction developed between the Swedish Nightingale and her American impresario.

After a little more than nine months on tour, Jenny Lind asked to be released from her contract and Barnum agreed. Her ninety-three concerts had earned almost $200,000 for her, and over $500,000 for the showman. Jenny married her German accompanist, retired to England and devoted her time to raising three children, singing only occasionally for needy causes.

When Jenny Lind died in 1887 at the age of sixty-seven, Barnum eulogized her by recalling how tender and comforting her glorious voice was and how much pleasure it had brought to so many people.

By the 1850's Barnum with his unique skills was the top-ranking showman in this country. He was a large hulk of a man with a robust air, a strong personality, often pompous, but considered by most to be a gentle and good-natured person. His bulbous nose, surrounded by thick folds of skin, provided a striking contrast to his clear, blue eyes. His sense of humor was limited, but he always enjoyed a good practical joke. He was better known for the platitudes which he not only frequently stated but firmly believed. His inflated ego was accepted as a vital component of success in the promotion business. Reading was one of his important hobbies. In his later years he wrote of his impressions and fantastic experiences as a show business entrepreneur.

In 1855 Barnum felt that he had worked hard enough to consider a prolonged rest and eventual retirement. He sold the museum, which had developed into a highly lucrative enterprise during the previous decade. He wanted to spend more time with his ailing wife, Charity, and their three daughters. He had built a pretentious mansion called Iranistan outside of Bridgeport, Connecticut. This was modeled after the oriental pavilion built for King George IV in Brighton, England. Architecturally grotesque, it suffered from an overabundance of turrets, spires,

James A. Bailey,
master circus man, joined
Barnum in 1880.

CIRCUS WORLD MUSEUM,
BARABOO, WISCONSIN

domes and latticework. The interior of the mansion was also ornately decorated with floors of imported marble, tapestries gracing the walls and sculpture from Italy. In this flamboyant retreat Barnum began writing his memoirs.

During this semi-retirement he was approached by a representative from the Jerome Clock Company in Bridgeport. The company wanted to move its plant to East Bridgeport— the town which Barnum was ambitiously trying to provide with adequate housing, parks and industry — if a certain sum of money were loaned to them during a temporary business slump. Barnum signed notes for bank loans which far exceeded the money he actually possessed. His association with the corporation turned out to be a fiasco, resulting in bankruptcy for the company as well as Barnum. The reputedly wealthy showman had to borrow heavily and go on tour with Tom Thumb to extricate himself. Shortly after resuming his role as director at the American Museum he learned that Iranistan had burned down. Fire would continue to plague the showman over the years.

In 1864, while this country was in the throes of the Civil War, Barnum became a member of a vigilante group trying to prevent sabotage. A Confederate plot had been conceived to set fire to many New York hotels, and a firebomb hurled at Barnum's museum almost destroyed the building. In July 1865 an accidental fire

broke out which leveled the American Museum. Bankruptcy and fires had dealt him shocking blows, but each time, like a phoenix arising from the ashes, Barnum renewed his determination to start over again. He opened his New American Museum in November 1865 at a new location and, having suffered no impairment of his magic as a showman, began to seek new vistas in entertainment.

Barnum opened a menagerie in New York under a canvas tent adjoining the museum. The collection included lions, tigers, giraffes, bears and a small elephant. Van Amburgh's menagerie was also added to form a huge animal complex. Barnum always made sure that the animals were well treated. When a member of the group (which later became the American Society for the Prevention of Cruelty to Animals) objected to some of the tricks the animals were trained to do, Barnum himself walked through a fiery hoop to prove that it could be done safely.

In March 1868, while on vacation at his seashore home in Connecticut, Barnum learned that the New American Museum had been destroyed by fire and was beyond salvage. The moment had come to give serious consideration to retiring. He was fifty-eight years old and knew that more leisure would allow him to travel and take a more active role in politics, which had always interested him. He was elected to a term in the legislature of his home state, Connecticut. Again in 1875, when pressures forced him temporarily to abandon show business, he became mayor of Bridgeport, serving one term. But the lure of the entertainment world still held him in its grip, and he succumbed once more to show business.

William Cameron Coup, a former roustabout and sideshow manager from Wisconsin, and Dan Castello, a former clown, asked Barnum to join them in the formation of a new

Iranistan,
Barnum's pretentious mansion
near Bridgeport, Conn.

circus and menagerie. Coup was confident that the prestige of the Barnum name and resources, coupled with his and Castello's experience, would prove a rewarding collaboration. The three partners opened a tent-circus in Brooklyn on April 10, 1871, calling it Barnum's Great Traveling Museum, Menagerie, Caravan, Hippodrome and Circus. Barnum, who had been mainly an exhibitor, was firmly launched as a circus showman.

Coup was made general manager and Castello, director of amusements, because of his past experiences as a concessionaire as well as a clown. Barnum's promotional genius took care of advertising.

With hundreds of animals and men the show performed successfully for a year. In 1872 it went out on its first railroad tour and traveled by night, sometimes more than a hundred miles to reach the next city by daybreak. W. C. Coup's creative mind devised the end-loading system of placing wagons aboard the train. He invented a ramp and rigging which pulled the circus wagons up into the railroad cars. A metal plate between each car allowed the wagons to be pulled along the entire length of the train.

Advance men put up brilliantly colored posters full of Barnum superlatives heralding the coming of the show. While the roustabouts were setting up the circus tents, elaborate circus wagons and animals paraded through the streets to attract customers.

Barnum was out of the country in 1873, purchasing animals for the menagerie collection, when he learned of his wife Charity's death. They had been married for forty-four years. Though she was a devoted and hardworking wife, she preferred to stay in the background of her famous husband's life. Ten months after Charity's death Barnum married Nancy Fish, an English girl forty years his junior. She was well-bred, vivacious

and possessed a fine sense of humor. Their marriage was a strong and happy one.

The 1870's began the Golden Age of the circus. The program in Barnum's show usually opened with a spectacular pageant, followed by new acts never witnessed before and including hundreds of performers and animals. The sideshow featured midgets, giants and "Fiji Cannibals." The menagerie had expanded to include barking sea lions in addition to the animals previously exhibited.

Winter performances were held in the Hippotheatron building in New York. When it was destroyed by fire in 1873, it became necessary to find larger and more permanent quarters. The Great Roman Hippodrome, which later became Madison Square Garden, was built for Barnum in 1874 at 26th Street and Madison Avenue.

At the end of the 1875 season when Dan Castello had already retired from the partnership, a conflict developed between Barnum and Coup which disrupted their relationship. Coup felt that the showman had permitted the Barnum name to be used indiscriminately by other circus companies. One in particular, John V. ("Pogey") O'Brien, was considered by Coup to be disreputable. With the departure of W. C. Coup, Barnum had to find a new manager. At this time he called on a circus syndicate, called the Flatfoots, which operated the circus for him from 1876-1880. During this time Barnum was mayor of Bridgeport, but he continued his zealous search for newer and greater attractions. In the season of 1880 he introduced a tattooed lady, a hairy-faced boy and "The First Human Cannonball, Mlle. Zazel."

James A. Bailey began an association with P. T. Barnum in 1880. This was to develop into the famous combination of names — Barnum and Bailey. A quiet and unassuming man, Bailey was precisely the

23

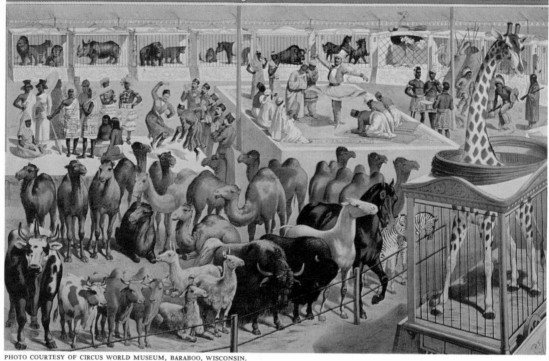

The Barnum & Bailey Greatest Show on Earth

opposite of Barnum in appearance as well as personality, but he was considered to be the real managerial genius behind the charismatic title.

Bailey had been a partner with James E. Cooper and James L. Hutchinson in the International Allied Shows combine, Barnum's competitors. Bailey, Cooper and Hutchinson were the first to use electricity in lighting their shows and capitalized heavily on this fact in their advertising. When the first baby elephant was born in captivity in an Allied show, Barnum offered them $100,000 for the baby pachyderm and its mother. When Barnum realized that they wouldn't sell this attraction, he asked that they join forces with him. Cooper had already withdrawn from the partnership, leaving only Bailey and Hutchinson. Their lengthy title included all of their inherited associations — P. T. Barnum's Greatest Show on Earth, Howes' Great London Circus, and Sanger's Royal British Menagerie. A huge parade took place in New York on March 16, 1881, to celebrate this partnership. The pageant included three hundred and fifty horses, twenty elephants, and fourteen camels, four brass bands, and almost four hundred performers.

For a brief period James A. Bailey withdrew from the partnership with Barnum, rejoining him in 1887 with a new contract which gave him full management of the operation and a fifty percent share of the profits. With Bailey's great efficiency and guiding spirit and Barnum's flare for the spectacular in advertising, which had earned him in previous years the title of the Shakespeare of Advertising, their circus evolved into the Greatest Show on Earth, one of the most spectacular and successful enterprises in circus annals. While some thought that the public would tire of circuses eventually, Barnum's response was that as long as there were children there would always be a circus.

In 1890, P. T. Barnum suffered a stroke which gradually weakened his formerly healthy state. In spring of the following year, when he knew that death was imminent, he asked to plan his own funeral and to read his own obituary in *The Evening Sun* in advance. On the day of his death, April 7, 1891, the greatest showman who ever lived weakly inquired about box office receipts of that day.

4
Charles S. Stratton

"General Tom Thumb"

Phineas Taylor Barnum's most successful promotion was a sprightly midget, Charles Sherwood Stratton. Introduced to the world as General Tom Thumb by Barnum, the twenty-five-inch midget took giant steps which catapulted him to fame and brought great fortunes to both of them. He was a personable little performer who charmed audiences around the world, including royalty and presidents as well as the common people, with his lighthearted songs and dances and quick wit.

Nowadays people understand and appreciate the hormonal deficiencies which occasionally result in physical abnormalities such as dwarfism, but this was not the case in the mid-1800's. Charles Sherwood Stratton was a true midget — a perfectly formed small person, born in 1838 into a family of normal-sized people. His growth was halted when he was only seven months old though he later increased in size. His weight at this time was only slightly over fifteen pounds.

Barnum heard of Charles Stratton when the youngster was five years old and living with his family in Bridgeport, Connecticut. Barnum's brother Philo was quickly dispatched there to speak with Mr. Stratton, a local carpenter, about the possibility of bringing young Charlie to see the director of the American Museum.

Mr. and Mrs. Sherwood Stratton were at first dismayed that their son was to be considered for Mr. Barnum's hall of human oddities, but then they conceded that perhaps it was an honor that the famous Mr. Barnum was interested in their little son. At the first meeting Barnum was completely won over by the tiny youngster. He renamed him General Tom Thumb after a character in the King Arthur legend. He advanced the boy's age to eleven and said that he came from England, believing that these statements would lend a certain mystique to the billing. Though

BARNUM MUSEUM
BRIDGEPORT, CONNECTICUT

the boy's mother was initially unreceptive to the idea of added years and shifting of her son's birthplace, she finally agreed.

Tom Thumb was an extremely shy child when he first appeared at the American Museum in 1843. With patient help from Barnum, he not only overcame his shyness but learned to speak with ease and to conduct himself in a gentlemanly manner. Though very young he seemed to possess definite theatrical talents and enjoyed learning little songs and dances.

Diminutive Tom Thumb got along very well with the husky six-foot-two-inch Barnum, and with a showman's instinct Barnum quickly recognized the career potential of his protégé. In addition to the songs and dances, Barnum taught him to do impersonations of Napoleon and Cupid, to tell little jokes in rhyme and wrote an introduction for him which started: "Good Evening, Ladies and Gentlemen; I'm only a 'thumb' but a good 'hand' in a 'general' way at amusing you . . ." This he used to open each performance. Tom Thumb was also

Below: Minute coach
built for **Tom Thumb** was pulled
by four Shetland ponies.

friendly with the other performers on the program — the acrobats and jugglers, but particularly the two giants, Goshen and Bihin, who appeared with him in his act. Above all, he loved the animal acts in the program.

When word of the midget's appearance spread, people were drawn like iron filings to a magnet. They flocked to see the "surprising and delightful General Tom Thumb." In the first fourteen months that he had appeared at the museum, more than eighty thousand people had come to see the twenty-five-inch wonder.

Barnum reaped a financial harvest by taking the celebrated elf on a tour of the principal cities along the eastern coast of the United States. This trip proved so successful that he immediately made plans for a European tour. Handbills and posters circulated by the clever entrepreneur read: "Last Chance To See General Tom Thumb Before He Leaves on His Great Journey!" Once again people formed in long lines for tickets.

In 1844 the great P.T. Barnum and his family, which included two young daughters, and the Strattons with their son set sail for Europe. Barnum was unsure of the kind of

CIRCUS HALL OF FAME, SARASOTA, FLORIDA

reception Tom Thumb might receive in a country as different from America as England, but as soon as they arrived Barnum hired a hall in which to present the General. Audiences quickly accepted the fact that this was no mere sideshow anomaly, but a charming, well-mannered and extremely talented young man. Above all, Barnum wanted to present Tom Thumb to Queen Victoria. The meeting was finally arranged and the eagerly awaited command performance was to take place in Buckingham Palace. A costume consisting of a brown velvet suit and a frilled white shirt were handmade for the midget, and a fancy plumed hat and a six-inch sword were added. Prince Albert, only three years old and just a few years younger than Tom Thumb, was to be among those present.

The songs, dances and impersonations were carefully rehearsed, and the cardinal rule when in the company of royalty was emphasized — always face the Queen, never turn your back to her. Tom Thumb remembered this royal custom and developed quite by accident his famous "ritual of withdrawing." After he had given his delightful performance, he and Barnum prepared to take leave of the Queen and her party. This had to be accomplished by making their exit across a broad gallery. For the long strides of Barnum this was not difficult, but for the miniature Tom Thumb this posed a problem. In order to cope with the situation he had to run a few steps, turn around and gracefully bow, then run ahead to keep up with his master, turn around and bow again, repeating this until they had both crossed the long room. Queen Victoria was charmed by this, and the sequence was repeated at all of his subsequent appearances.

While in England, one of Tom Thumb's greatest desires was fulfilled. Though he appeared to have a cosmopolitan deportment, he was still a six-year-old boy at heart who had

Wedding picture of
Tom Thumb and Lavinia Warren.

always wanted a live pony. In appreciation for the enormous success of their tour, Barnum generously had a miniature coach built for his child prodigy. The thirty-inch-high, nineteen-inch-wide carriage, which cost the showman several thousands of dollars, was handsomely decorated in red, white and blue with brilliant silver handles on its tiny doors. The interior was exquisitely made in every detail and was upholstered in a rich gold brocade. Venetian blinds shielded the windows. Four splendid white ponies pulled this superbly handcrafted coach.

In France, where the midget was known as Le Général Tom Pouce, he was widely acclaimed and was presented before King Louis-Philippe. The triumphal tour also included other countries on the European continent.

The enormous fortune which Barnum realized from Tom Thumb's appearances prompted him to draw up a revised lifetime contract in which the showman agreed to share equally with his little partner the profits from all of Tom Thumb's future bookings.

After the first tour of Europe, which lasted three years and included three command performances with Queen Victoria, the two travel-weary personalities returned to the United States. In the years following the illustrious General made repeated tours of the United States and Europe.

By the time he was twenty-three, Tom Thumb had grown ten inches and had become somewhat pudgy, but he never lost the magic of his appeal to audiences around the world. It was during one of Tom Thumb's tours that Barnum signed up another midget. She was a lovely twenty-two-year-old, thirty-two-inch tall former schoolteacher from Massachusetts named Mercy Lavinia Warren Bump which Barnum shortened to Lavinia Warren. When Tom Thumb returned and was introduced to her, he fell in love almost immediately. She

had been drawn, however, to another midget, named Commodore Nutt, also recently engaged by Barnum. A miniature version of the eternal triangle developed.

When Tom Thumb appealed to his mentor for help in this affair of the heart, the showman with his usual candor mixed with compassion, suggested that he would have to do his own courting. Tom Thumb successfully convinced Lavinia Warren that they should marry. On February 10, 1863, the two were wed in Grace Church in New York City. Their best man was Commodore Nutt, the rejected suitor. After the ceremony receptions were held in hotels in New York and Philadelphia. Thousands of people attended, and gifts of every description were bestowed upon the newly married couple. There was also a very distinguished reception held at the White House in Washington given by President and Mrs. Lincoln. When the lanky president was introduced to the groom, he shook hands solemnly and said, "General, here we have the long and short of it."

Tom and Lavinia were married for twenty years, but, although they had a good marriage, their union was never blessed with children. The world-famous midget, who had entertained millions of people, died of apoplexy in 1883 at the age of forty-five. A crowd of more than ten thousand came to his funeral. Although he had made millions of dollars in his lifetime, he had become extravagant in his tastes, losing his fortune and leaving Lavinia a relatively small inheritance.

Lavinia continued touring with another midget whom she married two years later. Before she died in 1919 her last request was that she be buried next to her first husband. The simple words, "His Wife," are inscribed on the tiny tombstone beside the monument of General Tom Thumb in the Bridgeport cemetery.

5
Jumbo

Mighty Lord of the Beasts

P.T. Barnum had always been an astute observer of audience reactions. One thing he was sure of was that they were fascinated by elephants. People came to see the color and pageantry of the circus, but elephants were what signified circuses in their minds. Perhaps this was one of the reasons why Barnum was more than routinely interested when he learned about the elephant Jumbo in England. The acquisition of this elephant was one of Barnum's greatest accomplishments. His wizardry in handling the advance publicity for this pachyderm provided so much free advertising that little had to be added by the showman.

Jumbo had come originally from Central Africa to France. The London Zoological Gardens received Jumbo from the Paris Zoo in trade for a rhinoceros. African elephants are supposedly difficult to handle, and Indian elephants are considered docile by nature and can be more readily trained. But Jumbo, an African elephant, was very gentle. He had carried children around on his howdah for seventeen years at the Royal Zoological Gardens in London.

Barnum learned that Jumbo was going through a "musth," a period in which male elephants are very irritable and impossible to manage, and that the London zoo keeper considered the possibility of destroying him. Barnum sent an agent to England with an offer of $10,000 to purchase the elephant. The offer was accepted by the zoo trustees over the loud objections of the British people. Londoners, including Queen Victoria and the Prince of Wales, were opposed to taking the pride of Britain away from his peaceful strolls around the zoo gardens. Exaggerated sentimentality encouraged by the press created an international uproar. To Barnum's pleasure both sides of the Atlantic regarded the affair as the most vital issue since the American Revolution. After a last ditch legal

effort to retain Jumbo failed and plans were made to transport him to America, it was the elephant himself who appeared most stubborn. He could not be coaxed to leave his familiar surroundings. A ruse had to be employed — a gigantic, heavily reinforced van was constructed with doors on either end through which the elephant walked several times. With careful timing the doors were closed when Jumbo was in the portable cage. He was now on his way to America. It cost Barnum $20,000 to transport the elephant.

Jumbo arrived on Easter Sunday in 1882, and the people were so anxious and curious to see the enormous animal which had caused such a furor in London that within two weeks time the initial investment was more than repaid to the showman. In six weeks time Jumbo brought in $336,000. At no time did he show signs of ill-temper. It is interesting to note that James Hutchinson, who was still in partnership with Barnum, objected to the purchase, claiming that an elephant was an elephant no matter what the size!

Jumbo was the largest captive elephant in the world when Barnum purchased him. He was twelve feet tall at the shoulders and weighed about seven tons. His trunk was twenty-seven and one-half inches in circumference and could reach an object twenty-six feet from the ground! His appetite was voracious! He consumed two hundred pounds of hay daily, plus several bushels of oats and other grains and several dozen loaves of bread in addition to vegetables and fruits. He drank countless buckets of water. His trainer, English-born Matthew Scott, was expert at handling him and traveled everywhere with him, for elephants need a great deal of special care. Their tender skin has to be rubbed often with softening emollients. Veterinarians also believe that elephants would probably do better with fewer peanuts

Engraving of Jumbo
exaggerates his size.
He was about twelve feet tall.

HARVARD COLLEGE LIBRARY, THEATRE COLLECTION

and popcorn and more fruits and vegetables.

Elephants were generally very useful in getting a circus show ready for presentation. They could haul and pull heavy equipment as well as help to raise and lower tents. But Jumbo was a show elephant, who led parades and entertained youngsters by giving them rides on his back.

On September 15, 1885, when Jumbo was twenty-five years old, the circus was setting up for a show in Canada. Jumbo and a smaller elephant, Tom Thumb, were walking along a railroad siding when an unscheduled freight train came speeding down the tracks directly in the path of the two animals. The engineer immediately signaled by blowing his whistle; he also jammed on the brakes, but it was too late. The engine rammed Jumbo against a circus train while the other elephant was thrown aside. The smaller elephant suffered only a broken leg, but Jumbo was killed in the accident. The locomotive and two cars were derailed and the engineer was killed.

Millions had seen and sat upon the back of Jumbo — one of the most famous of Barnum's attractions. In the three and a half years that Jumbo appeared in America he had made a fortune for Barnum and his partners. And a new word, meaning larger than normal, was added to the dictionary. The skeleton was sent to the American Museum of Natural History in New York for exhibit. The hide, weighing 1,538 pounds, was mounted on a wooden form. It is now on display at Tufts College in Medford, Massachusetts. Barnum never found an elephant to replace Jumbo. In fact no circus elephant since has managed to equal the drawing power of the colorful Jumbo.

6
Mollie Bailey

Everybody's Favorite Circus Aunt

I remember when "Aunt Mollie" used to sit on a rocking chair outside of her circus wagon in Texas, and the farmers would all come over with baskets filled with vegetables and fruits, eggs and milk, and she'd exchange the whole lot of them for tickets to her circus show. She'd have enough food for her own kids and all the circus help; the farmers would get in to see their "Aunt Mollie's Show" and everybody was happy!*

This unique woman — the only woman in circus history to own and operate her own circus show, and who was loved by all Texans for over half a century — was born in Alabama. Her journey from Mobile to the Lone Star state was long and intersected with many difficulties. Texans have always claimed her as their daughter since this show woman devoted most of her professional life to entertaining them.

Mollie Arline Kirkland was born of a sedate English father and a gentle French mother in 1841. The Kirklands were a family well-known and respected in Mobile. As Mollie matured, she developed into a raven-haired beauty, quick-witted, vivacious and admired by all who met her. Although trained in music from early childhood, she displayed a greater flair for dramatics and would frequently put on plays for her friends. When she was sixteen years old a touring circus troupe visited Mobile. Against the wishes of her stern father, who did not look favorably upon this form of entertainment, she attended the performance where she met James Augustus Bailey, a musician in the show, and immediately fell in love with him.

Mr. Kirkland did not approve of his daughter's association with the young circus musician and became more incensed when he learned that she intended to marry him. Mollie eloped with Bailey in 1858. The two returned shortly thereafter to attempt a reconciliation with her father and to ask for funds to start a small show of their own. Mollie's father firmly refused to accept the marriage and disowned her. Faced with this rebuff, Mollie "borrowed" a wagon and horse from his plantation and started out on a new life with her husband Gus.

With one horse, one wagon and abundant determination, the couple traveled along country trails from one small Alabama town to another. At each town they put on shows consisting of dramatic skits and pantomime which Mollie wrote and performed while Gus played various instruments. In those early years wagon-show travel was laborious. Adequate roads did not exist, and the existing horse trails were frequently muddy. But this hardy pair persisted, putting on their divertissements for the small-town audiences which

*Merle Evans, bandmaster of the Ringling circus in recent reminiscence about Mollie Bailey.

30

had a hunger for entertainment. The horse-drawn wagon would pull up to a schoolhouse where the Baileys would present a miniature vaudeville show with lighting provided by glimmering candles.

For several years Mollie and her husband continued to travel through the South with their simple, unpretentious little show, until the Civil War forced them to disband. Gus and Mollie joined Hood's Texas Brigade, leaving their year-old daughter with relatives. Gus became a soldier-musician and Mollie served as a nurse with the Confederate troops. She also sang for the soldiers when she could, but it was her unsung acts of heroism for which people remembered her.

Early in her tour of duty Mollie learned of the need for quinine in another Confederate camp. She volunteered to deliver it herself, carefully tucking the packets into the deep waves of her hair and covering it with a large hat. She made the risky journey on foot through unfriendly territory, arriving safely with the much needed quinine. Her talents as an actress were put to use when she consented to become a spy and, disguised as an old woman selling cookies, daringly went to an enemy camp to obtain information.

Once during this period with Hood's Brigade several horses escaped from their corral to a field near the encampment. One of them ate some green corn which made the horse ill, causing it to stagger around. Gus wrote down words describing what he saw, and a friend composed the music to the now well-known song: "The Old Gray Mare, She Ain't What She Used to Be."

One year after the war ended the Baileys returned to operating a circus show. They bought an old showboat, painted it with fresh, bright colors and traveled up and down the Mississippi River, stopping at the river towns to put on shows. Mollie always felt, however, that this way of living was really not suitable for raising her family. By that time she had four children — two girls and two boys. Mollie and Gus sold the showboat and went back to traveling through the South with their wagon show. In 1867 they decided to use the Houston area as a home base during the summer months, and it was here that the show was born which was to become a Texas institution—"A Texas Show for Texas People."

Within a few years the Bailey Concert and Circus Show grew into a one-ring tent show. A caravan of seven wagons was necessary to transport the added performers and small animal acts as well as the growing Bailey family, which had now achieved the balance of four girls and four boys! They journeyed all over Texas, and Mollie took careful note of the state of the crops along the way which might indicate local prosperity or lack of it. She was therefore able to gauge the potential success of their show at the various towns on their itinerary. But more than financial rewards, it was the sound of children's laughter which she most sought, for in Mollie Bailey's concept, "to live without laughter is not to live at all."

Travel along the poor roads was still the major problem, for it made arriving at a specific place on time difficult. They also had to contend with extremes of weather,

SAN ANTONIO PUBLIC LIBRARY, HERTZBERG COLLECTION

Painting of bareback riders
by W. H. Brown captures the flair
of the old time circus.

horse thieves, robbers and, at times, Indians! One night after the show was over and the tent had been rolled up, the travel-weary company settled down in the wagons, which were formed in a circle around the campsite. Suddenly a group of Indians appeared and surrounded them. Mollie quickly went around to the back of her wagon and started beating loudly on a drum. The Indians, frightened by the sounds which they thought came from a cannon firing from a nearby fort, fled swiftly from the circus camp. Many years later when Mollie met the Indian chief, who became one of her many close Indian friends, she recalled that night, and both of them enjoyed a hearty laugh over the incident.

New problems constantly plagued this circus family. Gus Bailey became ill and was no longer able to travel with the company. Then one of the young Bailey children died of food poisoning. During this time both of Mollie's parents passed away. Although Mollie and Gus had gone back to Mobile several times to attempt a reconciliation with her father and had even named one of their sons William Kirkland after him, the elder Kirkland never forgave her for marrying the circus musician. Mollie experienced many other personal problems and frustrations. She still managed to carry on with one thing she knew and loved best — providing entertainment for all the people.

When Gus Bailey's illness forced her to

take complete charge of the show in 1885, Mollie decided to make Texas their permanent home. Not only did she manage the circus and all of its complex logistics but she continued as a performer. The circus was renamed The Mollie Bailey Show. All of her children participated in the show. One daughter had a bird act and another daughter performed graceful ballet steps while riding bareback on a horse; her four sons contributed their talents as musicians.

The townspeople always looked forward with eagerness to the arrival of her show. Happy shouts of "Here comes Aunt Mollie!" echoed everywhere when the colorful wagon parade came down the main street. Mollie Bailey never advertised with the exaggerated claims that the larger circuses used. The people knew that her show would provide good, clean fun for the entire family. In the late afternoon between performances she would often walk around the town to do her marketing — a tall, graceful woman, shaking hands and greeting her many friends by name, while town youngsters danced along beside her. In one small town a merchant once teased her by asking, "When are you going to bring us a lion, Aunt Mollie?" "When I start charging a dollar. . . ." she retorted. She was known as the "Circus Queen of the Southwest," and they welcomed her back year after year. Children would be given the day off when the Mollie Bailey circus came to town. Her great love for people was demonstrated in many other ways. Orphans and soldiers were always admitted to her show without having to pay for tickets.

In addition to having a generous spirit, this extraordinary show woman was also quite astute and possessed shrewd business ability. She bought ground in the scattered towns where her shows were given, and at one time she owned over 100 lots in the state of Texas. Her circus layout was easily recognizable by the three flags which always hung above the main tent — the Union, the Confederate and the Texan banner. Mollie Bailey's lots were reserved for her circus during part of the summer months but were made available for baseball games, town meetings and other community projects once the tents were struck.

Gus Bailey died in Houston in 1896 during one of Mollie's tours. In the face of this great personal loss she resolved to carry on the tradition of her show. Around the turn of the century, when Mollie Bailey was in her sixties, she was still as vigorous as ever and eager to expand the horizon of her productions. She switched to railroads as the means of travel for her circus company. While recognizing the advantages of performing in the larger cities, she confessed that she missed her visits to the smaller towns where she had made so many friends. Her program had expanded to include a greater variety of acts and more performing animals. Although it was still a small circus company it modestly boasted an elephant named Bolivar, a camel and other animals, as well as tightrope walkers, acrobats and clowns. Her children continued to work with her. They "doubled in brass" as they also took care of the lots, handled advance publicity and performed many other activities to bring a show before the public.

At age seventy-seven Mollie fell and broke her hip. She never fully recovered from this accident and died in Houston on October 2, 1918. Her four sons tried to carry on, but the venture failed after two years. The Mollie Bailey Show became extinct. Mollie Bailey's credo of "do it right" and her emphasis on good clean amusement for all to enjoy were embodied in the shows she ran for so many years. She and her circus were fondly remembered by those who had known her.

7

The Ringling Brothers

Kings of the Circus Business

In 1869 when the floating *Paris Pavilion* of Dan Rice docked at the little river town of McGregor, Iowa, the five young sons of a local harness maker were among the people who welcomed the riverboat circus. As soon as the youngsters heard the steam calliope on the Mississippi River they quickly ran down to the docks to watch the unloading of the paddle-wheeled steamer and accompanying barge. Their excitement was further heightened when one of the troupe's performers came into their father's shop for some leather repairs, and circus passes for the family were given in exchange for the work. From then on the boys dedicated themselves to the idea of having a show of their own. Their first attempt at a circus show was made in 1870. The young men who ultimately became the Kings of the Circus charged one penny admission.

With scraps of old muslin and blankets for a tent, the five older sons put on a show in which the star attraction was a goat named Billy Rainbow. The boys displayed their versatility by playing various musical instruments, singing, dancing, juggling (with their mother's old plates!), acrobatics and a simple clown act. Albert (Al), the oldest son, was ringmaster. Their profits that season were $8.37. The next year admission was raised to five cents.

Albert, August, Otto, Alfred T. and Charles were the five older sons born to August and Marie Salome Rüngeling. There were also two younger sons, John and Henry, and one daughter, Ida, who was born later. The family moved to Baraboo, Wisconsin, and anglicized their name to Ringling — the name that was used in their first road show in 1882, grandiosely titled: The Ringling Brothers Classic and Comic Concert Company.

By 1884 the boys were so involved with circus entertainment that they convinced a famous veteran showman, Yankee Robinson, to join them in a new company they were forming. Yankee Robinson, born Fayette Lodawick Robinson, had owned one of the most popular circus companies in the midwest during the 1870's. Al Ringling had worked for him as a helper one summer and thought that Robinson's name would lend prestige to their new project. With the guidance of the unique circus proprietor, who had also been an actor, clown and dancer, the Ringlings acquired a more substantial tent and additional wagons which the young showmen embellished with novelty lettering and colorful paintings. The new show was called Old Yankee Robinson and Ringling Brothers Great Double Show, Circus and Caravan.

The parade which preceded the performance was led by the aging but still energetic Robinson followed by several wagons and a chariot bandwagon on which perched the Ringling brothers. Proudly the procession paraded down the streets of Baraboo. A dancing bear and a trained horse performed in the tent of this early Ringling enterprise. Al Ringling continued in his role of ringmaster and equestrian director. Otto beat the bass drum, John played his trombone, Charles bowed the violin, while Alf T. blew the cornet and led the band. The five Ringlings were also quick-change artists, dashing from bandstand to center ring and doubling as rope walkers, acrobats, jugglers and clowns.

Yankee Robinson quickly recognized the enormous talents and energies of these young men. The most prophetic words in circus history were probably uttered when he said that the Ringling brothers would someday become the greatest showmen in America!

At the end of their first season together, Yankee Robinson died at the age of sixty-six, but the Ringlings continued with the show for the next several seasons. They supplemented their incomes by concertizing with their Carnival of Fun during the winter months. They earned enough money to enable them to expand the number of wagons, purchase additional animals and to hire several new performers for their circus. After carefully studying maps of the nearby states, the Ringling brothers set out from Baraboo with a larger circus which they called: The Ringling Brothers Great Double Shows, Circus and Caravan and Trained Animal Exposition. The long and arduous journey over muddy trails was their greatest obstacle. They frequently had to hire people from little towns along the way to extricate the wagon wheels from the mud. The weary showman returned to Baraboo several months later with much practical experience, but no significant increase in their purses. Sheer willpower and determination made them continue in the exhilarating world of circus entertainment.

The Ringling brothers had gained enough know-how in circus matters to recognize the need for sending out an advance man to publicize the arrival of the show. John abandoned his clown costume and took charge of routing and advertising. Remembering the sage advice of Yankee Robinson, they never exaggerated unless they had something really worth shouting about. When a hyena was added to their growing menagerie, which consisted of a trained pig, a monkey and a bear, they billed the newest member as the "Hideous Hyena — Striata Gigantium!"

The Ringling brothers' ascent to fame in the following decade was phenomenal. The brothers had inherited from their father a deep sense of honesty and strong dedication to an ideal. These high standards contributed to their success. All of their profits were put back into the business and a withdrawal from the jackpot was made only for essentials. Majority rule was another policy which the Ringling brothers maintained. They also respected their mother's wishes when she asked that their shows never be performed

PHOTO COURTESY OF CIRCUS WORLD MUSEUM, BARABOO, WISCONSIN. USED WITH PERMISSION OF RINGLING BROS.–BARNUM & BAILEY COMBINED SHOWS, INC.

on Sundays. This Sabbath holiday and their penchant for honesty (unlike some circuses where professional pickpockets scattered among the crowds and shared their pickings with the management) caused the Ringling circus to be dubbed a Sunday school show.

Besides being frugal, the Ringlings were an intensely loyal and closely knit family. All seven brothers were now in the business and all worked well together as a team. Though on posters their faces looked alike, behind the black walrus mustaches there were many differences — both in appearances and in temperament.

When two elephants were added in 1888, the company went on tour under the title of the Ringling Brothers Greatest Show. Con-

35

Circus posters became
masterpieces of lithographic art
under the Ringlings.

PHOTO COURTESY OF CIRCUS WORLD MUSEUM, BARABOO, WISCONSIN.
USED WITH PERMISSION OF RINGLING BROS.—BARNUM & BAILEY COMBINED SHOWS, INC.

tinued success for the next two years allowed them to change their wagon show to a railroad show. The Ringling show which opened in 1890 traveled with more than a dozen railroad cars and presented their most spectacular production to date under a 170-foot rounded tent — quite an improvement over their mother's old muslin sheeting used not too many years previously.

By now the Ringlings had set aside their instruments and concerned themselves with management and production. (They continued to have an abiding interest in music throughout their lives.) Al was still equestrian director but was also producer and director of the show. Charles was in charge of logistics and was general manager. Otto handled the box office and finances. Alf T. was the public relations director, and John was in charge of routing the railshow. Gus went out in the advance car, and Henry, the youngest, manned the front door. With the unity and strength that came from shared responsibility the company moved ahead.

They played in all the small towns throughout the midwest in the early 1890's while Barnum was simultaneously staging his colossal "Nero and the Destruction of Rome" extravaganza in the east. By 1895 the Ringlings had invaded Barnum territory when they toured New England for the first time with a larger show than had ever been seen before. By 1897 they were using more than fifty railroad cars to move the circus on tour.

Meanwhile, James A. Bailey, the gentle, mild-mannered and efficient genius of Barnum and Bailey, had gone to Europe with one of the companies of the Greatest Show on Earth. When he returned after a successful five-year tour abroad, he found that the brothers from Baraboo had developed their show into serious competition for Barnum and Bailey. The Ringlings had expanded their show to include 400 horses, 300 circus performers and scores of trained animals. For the sideshow they had a unique museum of wonders. After his return Bailey countered by strengthening his own forces. For his first home show in 1903 he staged elaborate street parades which included the Two Hemispheres bandwagon, the largest and most ornate that had ever been built. A real clash was avoided however. The Ringlings and the Barnum and Bailey management realized that

Setting up the Big Top
was a smoothly run operation
involving teamwork and brawn.

running competing circuses was an expensive operation.

In 1905 the aging James Bailey sold the Ringlings a half interest in his Forepaugh-Sells Circus, giving the management of it to Henry Ringling. Thus the Ringlings and Bailey each ran their own shows, and each had a divided interest in the Forepaugh-Sells company. They mutually agreed that while touring each company would keep out of the other's territory. Bailey died the next year of complications from an insect bite, and the Barnum and Bailey company was sold officially to the Ringling brothers on October 22, 1907, for $410,000. The Ringlings eventually closed down the Forepaugh-Sells show so that there were only the two giant shows which traveled separately and in different geographical areas for the next several years. The Barnum and Bailey Circus was now commanded by John, assisted by Alf T. and Otto, while Charles and Albert ran the Ringling unit.

During the World War I years, travel, labor and other shortages along with the influenza epidemic made it increasingly difficult for the two companies to operate. By 1919 the two were consolidated into the largest circus in the world, and winter quarters were moved to Bridgeport, Connecticut.

By now the Ringling family of seven brothers had diminished to only two. Gus and Otto had died in 1907 and 1911, Albert in 1916, Henry in 1918 and Alf T. in 1919. At the time of the great merger into "The Big One," Charles and John were the only brothers remaining. The lone daughter in the Ringling family, Ida, had married Henry W. North around the turn of the century and had borne two sons, John Ringling North and Henry Ringling North. When Charles Ringling died in 1926, John was the last of the incredible Ringlings. It was the brilliant executive ability of "Mr. John," as he was always called, which

ALL PHOTOS CIRCUS WORLD MUSEUM, BARABOO, WISCONSIN

guided the Greatest Show on Earth to its zenith during the golden years of the twenties. Mr. John, considered to be the most powerful man in circus show business, poured all of his energies into this gigantic undertaking. During the early 1920's he increased the number of railroad cars traveling around the country to ninety-five. He had his own exquisitely appointed Pullman car. His personal knowledge of railroads was encyclopedic. It was said that he could take out his watch at midnight on any train trip and know exactly where they were at that precise moment.

As America moved into the twenties it became too heavy a task to organize street parades in addition to putting on a show in each city. Downtown areas had become crowded with automobiles, making it more difficult for the huge wagons to be pulled through them and return in time for the afternoon performance. So the popular and glorious street parades of the Ringlings passed into oblivion. But the programs which were offered had some of the greatest names in circus history. Featured in the shows in the twenties were: May Wirth, the famous Australian bareback rider; Lillian Leitzel, the fantastic aerialist; the Hanneford family of riders; the Wallendas and many other outstanding performers. Merle Evans, the bandmaster who joined in 1919, stayed for fifty years! While Mr. John held the reins of the mighty Ringling empire, he traveled around the world in search of the most unusual and exotic animals he could find. He stunned audiences by exhibiting the only one-horned Asian rhino and the first of several gorillas.

John Ringling was not only the mightiest circus magnate but also one of the richest men in the world. He owned oil wells, short line railroads and held mining interests. In 1927 he helped to develop Florida real estate by moving winter quarters from Bridgeport,

Connecticut, to Sarasota, Florida. Ringling had an avid interest in the civic matters of the little gulf town. He built a bank and hotel, helped to develop the St. Armand's Key area and built the first causeway across Sarasota Bay. But his consuming interest was in art. While he traveled through Europe in search of fresh new talent and extraordinary animals, he also purchased and added to his collection works of the baroque era and especially paintings by Rubens. A museum to house his admirable collection of paintings and sculpture and his own Venetian-style palace home, called Ca'd'Zan (John's house), were both completed by the late 1920's.

Both the complex world of the circus and his other interests demanded careful attention to detail. With his mind active in so many projects, John Ringling appeared to be a nervous man, somewhat high-strung and an habitual cigar chomper. Though he may have seemed somewhat formal in manner, he was extremely sociable and had many friends.

After many good years Ringling and his circus entered a period of trouble. When the Ringling Brothers circus was unable to schedule the engagement for the 1929 season at Madison Square Garden because of a dispute over Friday evening performances, the time slot was given to the Sells-Floto Circus. This was one of five smaller companies owned by the parent American Circus Corporation. By borrowing heavily, John Ringling purchased this conglomerate for two million dollars in order not to lose the Garden showplace.

The deal was barely signed when the stock market crash occurred. The country was soon in the throes of the Great Depression and receipts at the box office tumbled leaving John Ringling without cash to meet interest payments. In 1932 he suffered from a blood clot which weakened him considerably. That same year John Ringling lost control of the circus. The bank appointed a new manager,

Pageantry and exotic splendor
are, as always, an important part of
the magic of the circus.

Samuel Gumpertz, to run the show. This was the first time that a Ringling was not running the circus. At about the same time Ringling became pressed with divorce proceedings and income tax litigation. Although John Ringling had been heavily in debt, he permitted the sale of only three paintings from his fabulous collection to pay some of the bills. He had wanted to leave the museum as a legacy to the state of Florida. When John Ringling died in 1936, the circus that he helped to develop was fought over by his heirs. The complicated financial problems of Ringling's will and the various court actions took almost ten years to disentangle.

During the early 1930's the Ringling Brothers-Barnum & Bailey Circus exhibited for the first time a troupe of Ubangis, who wore plates in their mouths, as well as the strange-looking Burmese giraffe-necked women. Both of these unique attractions were widely advertised on posters. The famous animal trainer Clyde Beatty appeared with forty lions and tigers. The Zacchinis, the "Human Cannonballs," thrilled audiences of the thirties.

After John Ringling's death the sons of Ida Ringling North, Henry and John, borrowed enough money to regain control of the circus for five years. Under the stewardship of John Ringling North, who assumed the dominant role, greater and more outstanding acts were sought.

Stockily built, and resembling his namesake, John Ringling North worked briefly on Wall Street before being called upon to handle the business affairs of "Uncle John." When North took over as president of the circus corporation, certain of his habits induced animosity among various family members and the press. Despite his human frailties, John Ringling North managed his circus with determination. When his managerial career began, the circus was both physically and financially run down.

39

Within five years back debts were paid off. By the late thirties he had started to modernize the show. Utilizing the talents of well-known contemporary composers, choreographers, producers and designers, he improved upon the general format. The former helter-skelter sequence of acts was scrapped for a central theme around which all the acts were built. These changes were not welcomed by everyone. They felt that the more traditional aspects of the circus were being sacrificed in favor of a new "Broadway" aura.

Conflicts over policy differences continued to plague North. His on-again-off-again tenure with the circus which spanned several decades was punctuated almost from the beginning by frequent litigation involving various factions of the family and outsiders.

The star attraction during the North reign as owners of the Big Top was Gargantua, a fully grown gorilla who was billed as "the world's most terrifying living creature." The 550-pound ape was bought for $10,000 from a Brooklyn woman who used to keep him in her backyard! Though the Ringling nephews had purchased Gargantua, it was the publicity handled with great imagination and flair by the publicist, Roland Butler, which put the name of this huge beast in our vocabulary.

The late thirties showed the circus progress in strong and entertaining programs. The Flying Concellos and the Loyal-Repenskis were among some of the circus greats at this time. The next decade, however, brought new tragedies. In 1941 eleven elephants had died of accidental poisoning caused by spraying of chemicals on grass; in 1942 there was a musician's strike. But the worst disaster in circus history occurred in Hartford, Connecticut, on July 6, 1944. Control of the circus had passed from John North to other Ringling relatives in 1943 with the end of the five-year contract. The United States was at war and the entertainment industry of necessity had to use old materials trying to make the best of whatever they had. The fireproof hemp ropes they generally used were hard to obtain. The canvas tent had a paraffin covering which, though waterproofed, was not fireproof. Forty-one tents were on a lot near the town where only two water hydrants were accessible. Fire extinguishers which were normally available had not been unloaded after the previous engagement.

Over 8,000 people were in the tent that day when the show opened with the grand

Left: 1938 lithograph of Gargantua.

Right: John Ringling North.

Below: Ringling tented city
was put up for the last time in Pittsburgh
on July 16, 1956.

"spec." After the opening number, the clowns came out and entertained the audience while the Wallendas set up their dangerous high wire act. The show had been on for twenty minutes. A photographer standing in the wings spotted the first flames racing along the rope at the top of the tent. Fred Bradna, the ringmaster, gave his signal for the Wallendas to come down. Simultaneously Merle Evans, the bandmaster, switched to "The Stars and Stripes Forever," the traditional disaster music. An animal chute lying across the arena floor made an immediate escape impossible, and chaos resulted. Workers quickly made a chute so that those stranded in the top seats could slide down. Performers helped in every way possible. Despite all the heroic efforts of the circus men and performers, one hundred and sixty-eight men, women and children lost their lives and nearly six hundred persons were injured. Damage suits ran into the millions of dollars.

In the aftermath of this great tragedy it was necessary for the Ringling management to settle the claims with whatever means were at their disposal. Sorrowfully they managed to pull themselves together and carry on. In a few years the huge debts incurred by the tragic fire were paid off.

There were some changes in management in the following years. When John Ringling North returned in 1947 to assume control, he named Arthur Concello, a former trapeze artist, as manager. This energetic and highly creative former star was responsible for many contributions and innovations which not only made the circus a more handsome production but also helped streamline it economically.

By 1956 the handwriting on the canvas wall warned of the need for a momentous change. Increased costs of setting up the tents in different cities each day, growing labor difficulties, unavailability of suitable show lots and the inroads of television forced

John Ringling North to close the show in mid-season. In a dramatic speech in Pittsburgh on July 16 he announced that the days of the tented circus were over and that hereafter the big show would be played in indoor arenas. For those who decry the passing of the special sights, smells and sawdust of a bygone era, it should be remembered that the first circus was started by John Bill Ricketts in an amphitheater in Philadelphia.

John Ringling North, aware that ticket sales were unstable, and recognizing that there was no successor in the family, sold the circus in November of 1967. Judge Roy Hofheinz of Houston, who conceived and developed the Astrodome, and the Feld brothers, Washington theatrical promoters and booking agents for the circus, purchased the company for a reported $10 million. This sale brought to an end ninety-seven years of Ringling family control.

John Ringling North and Henry Ringling North now live in Europe. Though the North brothers have relinquished control of their beloved family circus, Henry remains as vice-president and consultant. He returns to the United States several times a year and generally may be found on opening night at Madison Square Garden watching the circus which bears his famous family name.

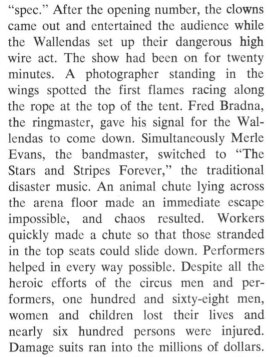

8
William F. Cody

"Buffalo Bill" — Pioneer Showman

The rugged frontiersman who brought the West to the East through the medium of the Wild West show was born on a farm in Scott County, Iowa, on February 26, 1846. The life of William Frederick "Buffalo Bill" Cody contained both heroic deeds and history-making events as well as many hardships. His early days as an Indian fighter, army scout and buffalo hunter were a continuous journey of exciting adventures. In his later life when he became a showman he was able to recapture the spirit of the American West.

When Bill Cody was eight years old his family moved to Kansas, where his father carried on trade with the Kickapoo Indians. There young Bill learned the language and customs of the Kickapoos from his friends among the children of the tribe. In his formative years he had little schooling, and his jobs varied from riding a mule as messenger for a freighting firm to looking after livestock on the Oregon Trail.

In 1860, at the age of fourteen he worked briefly for the Pony Express, carrying news and mail across the plains and mountains. Once, after he found intermediate stations along his route in ashes, he rode 300 miles, a record for the longest continuous stretch of riding. The relief riders had been killed by hostile Indians, who frequently ambushed passing stagecoaches and Pony Express riders.

During the Civil War William F. Cody served as a scout and guide for the Union Army. In 1863 he joined the 4th Kansas Cavalry and served as a private until the close of the war. In 1866, he married young Louisa Frederici in St. Louis. He appeared at the wedding in typical western dress — buckskin outfit, mustache, goatee and long, flowing blond hair. The father of the bride was certain that his new son-in-law was a bandit and an outlaw. Cody promised his wife that he would give up the plains and try to make a living at some other occupation, but, when an attempt

at running a hotel failed, he returned to the prairie and to the life he knew and loved best.

Cody's next job was with the Kansas Pacific Railroad killing buffalo to supply meat for the workers who were building roadbeds and laying rails. By his own estimate he shot and killed over 4,000 buffalo in the seventeen-month period he worked for the railroad. It was during this time that he earned the name of Buffalo Bill.

From 1868 to 1872 Cody served as a civilian scout for the military forces fighting Indians in the West, and he was awarded the Congressional Medal of Honor for gallantry in a fight with Indians on the Platte River. Cody's career as a scout attracted the attention of a writer, Ned Buntline. Buntline (E.Z.C. Judson) made him the hero of a dime novel published in 1869. It was later dramatized and in 1872 Buffalo Bill became the leading actor in the stage version. Cody broke with Buntline the next year but his acting career lasted for eleven seasons. In 1876 he took leave from the stage to rejoin the 5th U.S. Cavalry as chief scout. He served under General Custer fighting the Sioux and Cheyenne Indians until Custer was killed in a battle with the Sioux. In a skirmish a week after the Battle of Little Big Horn Cody killed a Cheyenne leader, Chief Yellow Hand, in a duel.

Cody realized with the passage of time and the fading of the frontier that his days as a scout were almost over. Inspired by the success of a July 4th Frontier Day celebration he had organized at North Platte, Nebraska, he began thinking of a western show which would be staged out-of-doors. There, as he mentioned in his autobiography, "the horses could be ridden at full gallop; lassos could be thrown; and pistols and guns fired with safety." The performance could not take place in a regular tent because the poles and rigging would obviously interfere with the action. Instead Cody used an open-air arena surrounded by shaded grandstands. He assembled a large group of Indians, cowboys and stagecoach drivers and put on his first spectacle of western adventure in Omaha in May 1883. To the rodeo-like acts of riding and roping he added a mock battle with the Indians and reenactment of a stagecoach hold-up. The show was an immediate success.

A typical Cody Wild West Show began with Buffalo Bill leading the parade of top cowboys and Indian riders around the arena. The Indians, friendly chiefs and braves brought in from the reservations, performed tribal dances and war chants before their wigwam village. The big number, of course, was the staged Indian attack against a wagon train and the rescue by cavalry and Buffalo Bill. Adding to the excitement and colorful events were the famous sharpshooters, the Bogardus family.

Because of the novelty of this kind of show, people thronged to the arena and Buffalo Bill became quite prosperous. Two years later, in 1885 while the show was on tour, a nineteen-year-old girl joined the company. Her name was Annie Oakley. She performed feats of marksmanship with a rifle unparalleled by any other woman of the time. Her special stunt was lying on the back of a galloping horse and shooting glass balls that were tossed into the air. Another skilled shooter who appeared regularly with the Wild West show was young Johnny Baker. Buffalo Bill took this lad under his wing as a foster son after his own son, Kit Carson Cody, died at the age of six.

Cody toured successfully with the Wild West show for three years. In a letter from Mark Twain, the noted writer suggested he take the show to Europe since it distinctively represented the American West. Mark Twain felt that Europeans could learn much about our country through Cody's entertainment.

In 1886 Cody sailed on a chartered ship for England. The Indians traveling with him were at first frightened by endless days of seeing

BROWN BROTHERS

nothing but water, but Cody reassured them. When they finally landed the Indians were relieved to discover they were not going to fall over the edge of the earth.

Arriving in England Cody made arrangements to stage the show in an amphitheater which had a circumference of one-third of a mile. The show began with a grand march, followed by war dances and chants, then moved along to the spectacular staging of battles. The initial performance was given for the Prince of Wales, who later became Edward VII of England, and Princess Alexandra. Afterwards at a command performance for Queen Victoria, Chief Red Shirt, a chieftain participating in the show, was introduced to the Queen. A look of pride was noted on the chief's face for here was one ruler meeting another. When a second command performance was given, the Prince of Wales suggested that his guests be allowed to ride on Cody's prize exhibit, the Deadwood stagecoach. Cody then escorted the kings of Saxony, Denmark, Belgium and Greece around in a breathtaking ride while blank shots were fired by the Indians, who had been told to

43

Young Buffalo Wild West Show
set-up typified open arena
preferred by such shows.

CIRCUS WORLD MUSEUM, BARABOO, WISCONSIN

whoop it up for this special ride. When the ride ended, Cody told the Prince of Wales, seated beside him atop the coach, "I've held four kings before, but this is the first time I've ever played the royal joker!"

Several years later, when Cody again visited Europe with his Wild West show, he played for audiences in Spain, France and Italy. Cavalrymen from many different countries were recruited for his shows back home. In Italy at the Vatican, Cody met Pope Leo XIII at the papal coronation ceremonies to which his entire company had been invited. In Rome it was also suggested that the Wild West show be performed in the Colosseum. But Cody claimed that the famous structure and its inside arena were too small!

Dr. W. F. Carver, a former dentist and skilled marksman, joined Cody in some of his early ventures. Nathan Salsbury, an actor turned showman, shared a more lasting association with Cody. In 1894 James A. Bailey, who had joined Cody and Salsbury, utilized some of the equipment remaining from the sale of the Forepaugh-Sells show which Bailey had formerly operated. (It is interesting to note that the Ringling brothers never particularly cared for cowboy and Indian presentations and rarely included them in their format.) In 1895 the organizational genius Bailey prepared Cody's show for railroad travel, making possible one-night stands.

In 1906 Bailey died, and a year later one of Cody's competitors, Major Gordon W. Lillie (Pawnee Bill), bought out Mrs. Bailey's interests. The new show was called Buffalo Bill Wild West and Pawnee Bill Great Far East Show. Lillie's association with Cody for a time helped ease some of his growing financial problems, for Cody was more extravagant than he should have been. He had earned millions but had spent it as fast as it came in. With Lillie's help, Cody hoped to put on the finest spectacle ever known.

The program for the combined show listed the following events: Introduction of the Congress of Rough Riders of the World; A Review of various Indian tribes; The Occident meets the Orient; U.S. Cavalry veterans; Australian bushmen; Cossacks; Hindu Fakirs; A Buffalo hunt; A Virginia reel on horseback; Marksmanship contests; Deadwood stagecoach sequence. This elaborate show, however, did not meet expectations. 1911 was the worst year in terms of bad weather and low gate receipts. Cody tried to recoup some of his losses by strengthening the show and advertising it as a farewell tour the following year, but the show continued to lose money.

The almost legendary frontiersman who had always been known for his nerves of steel and great physical fortitude was beginning to show signs of wear and fatigue. Though his robust manner of living included an occasional drinking spree, he had enjoyed rugged good health throughout most of his years. Cody's philosophy, which echoed his almost limitless energies, is illustrated by the following remark:

When a man is engaged in work on the plains he forgets all about the wear and tear on his system and not until all danger is over and he is safely resting in camp does he begin to feel what he has been through. Then a good night's rest usually puts him all right again.*

At this time a good night's rest and some additional capital were no longer able to help Cody. He had made great fortunes during his fantastic career, but soon rival circus companies with their more daring acts and even better performers began making inroads. Cody next turned to making Indian war films — a venture which did not prove successful. After a brief stint with the Sells-Floto Circus, Cody was hired by the 101 Ranch Shows, an ironic twist of events for a man who had once

*William F. Cody, *An Autobiography of Buffalo Bill.*

44

Deadwood stagecoach sequence
is featured on this 1908 poster
for Buffalo Bill's Wild West Show.

PIONEER PERILS IN THE EARLY DAYS OF THE ORIGINAL DEADWOOD STAGE COACH
AN ATTACK BY HOSTILE INDIANS AND RESCUE BY THE COW BOYS

PHOTO COURTESY OF CIRCUS WORLD MUSEUM, BARABOO, WISCONSIN.
USED WITH PERMISSION OF RINGLING BROS.—BARNUM & BAILEY COMBINED SHOWS, INC.

owned his own show. He was then close to seventy-one years of age.

Because of previous unwise speculations and other debts he had incurred, Cody was bankrupt. He tried to interest a mail-order house in selling prints of his portrait done years earlier by Rosa Bonheur. This also failed. He then applied to the War Department for the ten dollars a month paid to holders of the Congressional Medal of Honor. The man, once a millionaire, now desperately needed the ten-dollar dole. (After his death his name was struck from the roll because Cody had been a civilian when the medal had been awarded.)

Though he continued to work for several months with the 101 Ranch Show, his strength was slowly ebbing. He died on January 10, 1917. His tomb, blasted from solid rock on Lookout Mountain near Denver, Colorado, looks out on the vast plains over which he rode for so many years.

The dream of William F. Cody had been realized in his lifetime. He had presented to the world a vivid picture of the vanishing plains with their many dangers as well as their romanticism. He may have exaggerated the adventure of the West for his shows and stories, but his exploits as a hunter and scout are unquestioned. And as a personality and showman he certainly was unique. Variations of those early Rough Rider shows may still be seen in some contemporary circuses and commercial "Wild West" exhibitions.

9
Annie Oakley

"Little Sure Shot"

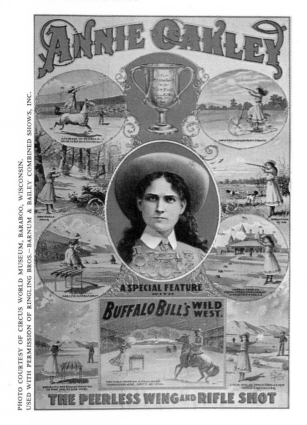

Annie Oakley's name, her lovable traits and her thoughtful consideration live as a mark for any woman to shoot at.*

When the famous Bogardus family of marksmen retired from the Buffalo Bill Wild West Show a dainty, petite woman quickly filled the gap. Annie Oakley, one of the world's most accurate woman sharpshooters, had been born Phoebe Anne Oakley Mozee on August 13, 1860, in a log cabin in Darke County, Ohio. Young Annie, a tomboy who was small for her age, began shooting a rifle when she was nine. After her father died she helped to support the family by hunting and trapping small game to sell at the local market.

*Will Rogers in 1926. Fenner and Fenner, *The Circus; Lure and Legend*.

Her skill with a rifle was quickly recognized, and she gained a reputation for marksmanship among her friends.

A team of touring professional marksmen appeared at the Cincinnati Opera House when Annie was about fifteen years old. She entered a rifle shooting contest held on the stage of the theater. She fell in love with the expert rifleman she defeated, Frank Butler, and married him one year later. Their early years of marriage were spent in vaudeville variety shows, appearing in tandem, though Annie always had star billing on the program. In later years Frank Butler acted as her manager. When Annie was told that she needed a stage name, she chose the family name Oakley because she liked the sound of it and thereafter she was known as Annie Oakley.

Frank Butler and Annie Oakley joined the Sells Brothers Circus in 1884 when they learned of an opening in that group. During the short period that she worked for this circus she developed her famous act of shooting moving objects from the back of a galloping horse. While her husband tossed colored glass balls high into the air, Annie with precision and grace, shot each one as she continued to ride around the ring. The costume she wore in those early shows became her trademark—a wide-brimmed cowgirl hat, pleated skirt and leggings.

While touring as a featured star in the Sells Brothers Circus, Annie met Buffalo Bill Cody whose Wild West Show was performing at the same time in New Orleans. The show people exchanged visits as was the custom then, and Annie was so impressed with the congeniality of the Buffalo Bill company that she asked for employment for both herself and her husband. The Butlers had not been particularly pleased with working and living conditions at the Sells Brothers Circus and were eager to make a change. Buffalo Bill

Gun used by Annie Oakley.

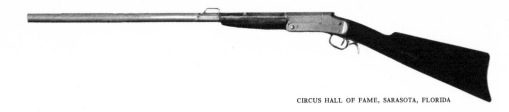

consented to hire them, and they joined the Wild West Show in Louisville where the Bogardus family played their final performance. Annie Oakley and the famous frontiersman shared a warm friendship in these early days. He assured her that she could stay with the show "as long as you like, Little Missy," his own pet name for her.

Buffalo Bill scheduled Annie Oakley's shooting exhibition after the opening number of his show. He reasoned that when the females in the audience saw the tiny woman handling guns with such ease they would be less frightened by the loud noises of the mock battles which followed her on the program.

Sitting Bull, whose tribe had fought against Custer a few years previously, was appearing in the Buffalo Bill Wild West Show at that time. He had returned from exile in Canada to work for Cody, his former enemy, now his friend. Audiences were fascinated not only by the rich and colorful history of this former medicine man but by his appearance and bright costume, which included a brocaded waistcoat! Old Sitting Bull added to Annie's growing list of nicknames by calling her "Little Sure Shot." Annie Oakley was also honored by being adopted into the Sioux tribe.

Every one of Annie Oakley's performances with the Wild West Show was well attended. Though Buffalo Bill was an accomplished sharpshooter, it was the diminutive Annie Oakley whom the people came to see. In a single day she had once shot 4,772 out of 5,000 glass balls that were tossed into the air for her. Among other stunts which she perfected and which helped win acclaim for her was the ability to hit the thin edge of a playing card from a distance of ninety feet. She would then proceed to puncture the card with additional shots as it fell to the ground. This trick enshrined her name in circus lingo. Cards that were holed by her rifle shots became treasured for their souvenir value and were called "Annie Oakleys." Subsequently all punched tickets used as circus passes became known by that name.

During those triumphant years with Buffalo Bill, Annie Oakley had never been happier. She often entertained the young children of the performers, yet she was equally at ease with the rougher, more virile horsemen. Everyone loved her. In some of her spare moments she coached young Johnny Baker, Bill Cody's foster son, and gave him advice: "Practice, practice, practice, and always believe in yourself. Don't try too hard, though, or you'll get too tense. Coordination is the important thing!" This she felt had been responsible for her own success.

When Buffalo Bill's troupe toured Europe in 1887 it was warmly greeted. At Annie Oakley's first command performance before Queen Victoria, the charmed royal dowager exclaimed, "You are a very, very clever little girl."

The first of several seemingly minor differences occurred between Cody and Annie Oakley during this overseas trip. When Buffalo Bill learned that Annie Oakley shook hands with the Princess Alexandra rather than bowing and kissing the back of her hand, he was visibly upset by what he considered a breech of etiquette toward royalty. He took offense that his protégé had offered a hand that was "somewhat shaded with gunpowder." Moreover, in a shooting match against Grand Duke Michael of Russia, who fancied himself to be an expert marksman, Annie defeated this royal personage, further displeasing Buffalo Bill. A coolness developed between Cody and Annie based partly on these incidents.

Annie Oakley was in constant demand during their stay in England, not only as a performer in the show but also to give shooting lessons to society women, who

Below: Annie Oakley achieved fame with her trick of shooting glass balls from the back of a galloping horse.

considered it quite fashionable to copy her clothing style. Her dressing tent was always filled with flowers from admirers. The Prince of Wales presented her with a medal and they exchanged photographs. The over-whelming popularity of the dynamic little star undoubtedly awakened jealousy in Buf-falo Bill and added to the growing estrange-ment between the two. Friendship seemed to have won out over performer sensitivities for she stayed with the show. Cody later wrote in Annie's diary while they were touring Germany, "To the loveliest woman both in heart and aim."—signed W.F. Cody, Strass-burg, 1890.

While the show was entertaining audiences in Germany, Annie was invited by Crown Prince Wilhelm to give a private shooting ex-hibition in Berlin. He asked that she perform with him a stunt he had seen her do before — to shoot the ashes from a cigar he was holding in his mouth. Her shot was only four inches away from the future Kaiser's face. The story goes that some years later, in 1917, Annie wanted to write him a note asking for another opportunity to have a shot at his cigar.

When the troupe finally returned to

America in 1892 it spent the entire winter preparing for the Chicago World's Fair of 1893. The show was renamed Buffalo Bill's Wild West Show and Congress of Rough Riders of the World, for many cavalrymen had been recruited from the countries visited on the tour abroad. But Annie Oakley still remained a sensation of the show. At this time she added a trick to her act, delighting audi-ences by shooting at moving targets while rid-ing a bicycle around the ring. The country seemed to have Oakleymania! Many articles of clothing and objects were named for her.

After many years of extensive traveling Annie expressed a longing for the peace and solitude she felt she had missed over the years. She wished for a life with a slower pace, in which she could settle down with her husband and take up needlework.

On a final "farewell tour," she was in an unfortunate train crash in which she was severely injured. In 1911 an automobile accident again incapacitated the once active and great markswoman. By the time of World War I she had recovered sufficiently to tour army camps with her husband where she put on sharpshooting exhibitions for which she refused remuneration.

In her twilight years she continued to enjoy many warm friendships. Will Rogers, a former neighbor, visited Annie as she lay ill in bed during her final days. He felt inspired to write a letter to a newspaper which summed up his feelings about this great woman: "Annie Oakley is one of the finest and truest American women. . . .I have heard cowboys who traveled with her speak of her in almost reverence. . .It's what you are, and not what you are in, that makes you."

On a chill November evening in 1926, frail, white-haired Annie Oakley, who will always be remembered for her proficiency with a rifle, died peacefully in her sleep. Her hus-band's death followed three weeks later.

10
Lillian Leitzel

Mercurial Queen of the Aerialists

Lillian Leitzel was temperamental, demanding and unpredictable. She threw temper tantrums of volcanic proportions. She dismissed people who crossed her by shrieking curses at them in a variety of languages — a verbal outburst which frequently was accompanied by a slap of her right hand. Yet when visitors come to the Ringling Museum of the Circus in Florida forty years after her tragic death and see the swivel ring from which she fell, their eyes become moist and their throats choke up. The hypnotic appeal of this tiny woman aerialist, whose changes of mood made her violent one moment and lovable the next, was unmatched by any other performer in the history of the circus. She possessed a flamboyance which endeared her to audiences despite her numerous peccadilloes. In brief she was utterly fascinating.

The undisputed queen of all aerialists in the early part of this century was born Lillian Alize Pelikan Eleanore in Breslau, Germany, in 1882. She was called Leitzel, a diminutive of Alize. In later years she took this nickname as her stage name. Her mother's family boasted a long heritage of skilled circus performers — her grandmother was still able to swing on a trapeze at age 84! One of Lillian's uncles originated the famous plank trick which is still used in circuses today — a board balanced on a clown's head remains undisturbed even after the clown walks briskly in one direction, then suddenly turns about-face and walks in the other direction with the plank still resting on his head. Lillian's mother, Elinor Pelikan, and her mother's two sisters were famous and popular trapeze artists in Europe. They were known as the "Leamy Ladies" — named for their American manager, Edward Leamy.

Lillian inherited an acute sense of daring from her Czech-born mother. Her father, a former Hungarian army officer, later gave himself the imposing title of "Impresario" when he fancied he could manage the family's show appearances. He was a strict disciplinarian whose rigorous and demanding practice sessions with the family were not unlike his training of army troops; an attitude which later caused the marriage of Lillian's parents to be dissolved.

Lillian and a younger brother were reared in Breslau by their maternal grandparents, since their mother was away from home traveling with the Leamy Ladies act during much of their childhood. However, the children's mother always insisted that they get the best possible education. At school both children showed outstanding talent for literature and languages. Lillian spoke five languages fluently. She also attended conservatories in Breslau and Berlin where she studied dancing and music. For a time the family thought that Lillian might become a concert pianist, but, while she loved music, her mischievous spirit interfered with her lessons — she once stood on her head while trying to play Chopin. In spite of such adolescent larks she maintained an interest in music, art and ballet throughout her circus career.

As a young child Lillian often enjoyed watching her mother and her aunts perform their graceful trapeze act high in the air. She was only nine years old when she showed her mother some tricks which she had taught herself on a small trapeze and expressed a childlike desire to travel with the Leamy Ladies act. Although her mother initially disapproved, Lillian, when older, joined the famous act and toured Europe for several seasons before coming to the United States with them in 1910. Though the troupe had been enormously successful in Europe they were not as well received in this country. The Leamy Ladies returned to Europe, but Lillian, now in her twenties, remained in the United States to try her luck as an aerialist working alone.

Tiny Lillian Leitzel, who was only four feet nine inches tall and weighed less than one hundred pounds, longed to be a great aerial star but the only bookings which she could get at that time were in vaudeville shows. Her first accident occurred in a theater in New Jersey. Lillian's legs were hurt in a fall, but with her plucky spirit she insisted on returning to work on crutches. When she came back to the show, she had to be carried to the "web" or rope that hung from the ceiling. Once at the web she climbed to the top quickly and smoothly as if nothing had ever happened. She went through her routines gracefully on the Roman rings at the top of the theater, then glided down the web to be greeted by thunderous applause from the audience. Lillian was on her way to stardom. She demanded and received a salary greater than that given to any other performer. She was soon billed as "Lillian Leitzel, the World's Most Daring Aerial Star."

In 1915 while appearing in a vaudeville show in South Bend, Indiana, an agent of the Ringling Brothers Circus spotted Lillian Leitzel and at once recommended her for the Big Show. By the time of the great merger between Barnum and Bailey and the Ringling Brothers shows into one circus in 1919, Leitzel's fame had grown to the point where she was the reigning queen of the circus, and her salary which had begun at $250 per week had begun to climb even higher. She had top billing and her act was given center ring prominence. But, along with stellar status, the caprices of her personality were emerging. Lillian's aerial presentation generally lasted eight minutes. If she felt inclined to lengthen it to heighten the drama, she would do so. In a circus show whose acts must be closely timed this frequently created problems. Nevertheless she would often sit on the rings or hang on a rope from her lofty position at the top of the tent and wave and giggle at the audience for a long time. If she had recently feuded with a roustabout she might stay up there and make grimaces at him. The audience loved this little display and never objected to waiting for Leitzel to resume her act.

Her flair for the dramatic was evident as soon as she entered the ring. The house lights dimmed as one lone spot was directed onto the tiny aerialist. Instantly the audience

50

CIRCUS WORLD MUSEUM,
BARABOO, WISCONSIN

felt Leitzel's magnetic presence. To empha-size her smallness, a giant in a doorman's costume often carried her out to the center ring. Her personal maid, Mabel Clemings who was also rather tall, occasionally ac-companied the two and stood by to accept her robe. Lillian Leitzel's costumes were glittering creations, often accentuated with expensive jewelry.

She began her act by climbing up the web to the top of the tent. Her ascent was smooth and effortless. It appeared as though she "rolled" herself up the length of the rope until she reached the top where the Roman rings hung. She then performed intricate twists and turns, ending with a handstand on the rings. With equal grace she slid down again, thus ending the first half of her act.

The most awe-inspiring part, requiring un-limited amounts of physical endurance, came next. The audience was stilled; no candy butchers were allowed to peddle their wares. Leitzel climbed up a separate web. She slipped her right hand and wrist through a padded rope loop which was attached to a swivel and ring. Then she threw herself over and around in a series of swing-overs or one-arm planges, accompanied by the roll of snare and bass drums as the audience counted each flip aloud, up to one hundred or more. Once, in a burst of bravado, the sensational little Leitzel twirled around for a record 249 times! Generally, she executed around 100 turns, and in her later years about 60 flips. She developed great style in her performance but she was also quite fussy. If she did not find the adjustment of the rope to her liking she would fly into a wild rage; or if the drummer didn't produce the correct roll sound he was told off in the most explosive terms.

The pinwheel gyrations which appeared so easy took their toll on the artist. Every time Leitzel did the one-arm planges, her right shoulder became partially dislocated but then snapped back. Her wrist caused her constant pain, and though numerous wrist guards were tried, none were successful. She was also quite self-conscious about the appearance of her wrist and would camou-flage it with long sleeves, ornamental brace-lets or a casually worn chiffon kerchief. Her series of planges required great muscular strength and resulted in overdeveloped arms and shoulders which did not seem to belong to her otherwise minute frame and narrow waist. Her legs were slim and her feet were so tiny that she wore a child-sized shoe! Though she was not beautiful by most stan-dards, she was attractive in a merry, pert way that made her quite appealing.

The public worshiped Leitzel. They savored the morsels of information, often inaccurate, which she furnished newspapermen when they interviewed her. The people with whom she worked remembered her histrionics almost as much as her enormous talents. Her maid was fired and rehired at least four times a day, then was showered with gifts and money.

She was very popular with men and had many suitors who bestowed expensive furs, jewels and other gifts upon her. She seemed to cast a hypnotic spell on them, but at the same time she preferred to keep them guessing. She adored the children of other circus performers, and, perhaps because she had been starved for affection in her own childhood, she lavished attention on them. Their birthday parties were always held in "Auntie Leitzel's" own dressing tent, which had elegant furnishings and draperies and fresh flowers everywhere. If the show was on the road Leitzel invited the children into her private Pullman car, which contained a baby grand piano. There she entertained them with songs in different languages and stories remembered from her own childhood.

At the height of her career Lillian Leitzel

51

Star-crossed couple,
Lillian Leitzel and Alfredo Codona.

married a fellow performer whose artistic temperament resembled her own—handsome, brilliantly talented Alfredo Codona, the "King of the Trapeze." His English mother and his Mexican father were both from circus families. With his father and brother he appeared in a trapeze act in different countries before coming to Ringling Brothers Circus in 1917. He was famous for his triple somersault which required not only tremendous skill but precise timing. His manner of performing this difficult feat verged on recklessness.

Leitzel's friends felt that the impassioned marriage was inevitable — these two highly volatile personalities were destined to be attracted to each other. Perhaps it was similarly ordained that the lives of these two daring and reckless lovers would each end tragically. After a stormy courtship marked by jealousies, battles and apologies, Lillian Leitzel and Alfredo Codona were wed in Chicago in 1927. The ceremony was highlighted by the three-hour absence of the irascible bride. Considering the temperaments of the two, the marriage was a good but strange one.

During the winter months when the circus was not on tour, Alfredo and Lillian played engagements at various theaters in America and Europe. On February 13, 1931, Lillian was appearing at the Valencia Music Hall in Copenhagen, Denmark, while her husband was under contract to perform at the Berlin Winter Garden. Lillian had finished the first half of her act on the Roman rings and was preparing for the final half consisting of planges on the swivel ring. She climbed swiftly to the ceiling as she had done thousands of times before. As she started this part of her act, suddenly the swivel ring snapped. The metal had crystallized through the constant heating and cooling of the ring caused by her turns, and she fell twenty feet to the ground landing on her shoulders and back. She tried to get up as she insisted, "I'm all right, I can go on." She was overruled and taken to a hospital. Alfredo Codona was notified in Berlin and rushed to her bedside. Her husband's visit seemed to bolster her spirits considerably, and she convinced him to return to Berlin to complete his engagement. On Sunday morning, February 15, 1931, the greatest woman aerialist died of a concussion and complications resulting from her fall.

Lillian Leitzel was a superb aerialist, whose mercurial personality made her the most talked about circus performer of her era. Early in her career when asked why she would want to subject herself to this torturous aerial act, she had replied, "I'd rather be a race horse and last a minute than be a plowhorse and last forever."

Leitzel's tragic death caused the grieving Codona to become more reckless than ever before in his performances. He almost completely abandoned the necessary precautions on the trapeze bar. After a fall in which he tore the ligaments in his shoulder he was forced to retire permanently from "flying." He had married another circus performer, but their life together was marked by unhappiness. When this marriage was about to be terminated, Codona was asked by his wife to meet with her at her lawyer's office. Codona appeared but then asked to be left alone with his wife. He pulled out a revolver, shot her and killed himself — a murder and suicide which shocked the circus world and the public.

11
Clyde Beatty

Fearless Trainer of the Big Cats

The risk of danger and chance of accident to a wild animal trainer are always great. The secret of remaining unscathed, according to one of the world's most renowned animal trainers, Clyde Beatty, was in establishing dominance. Beatty learned early in his career that a trainer had to act with authority and at the same time show respect and understanding for the animals he faced. Only then, he claimed, are you able to make the primitive beasts respond to training. This sounds sensible and easy enough except that it means facing down a number of snarling cats, each weighing 300 to 400 pounds and ready to take off your head or an arm if given a chance.

Clyde Beatty was only seven years old when the circus came to his home town of Bainbridge, Ohio. The caged Royal Bengal tiger so impressed the youngster that he put on his own "wild animal show." This included a dog, a cat, some guinea pigs and a raccoon which he taught a few simple tricks. But the child's ultimate dream was to work with and train fierce beasts like those he had seen at the circus show.

When he was sixteen years old, Clyde Beatty ran away from home and worked with a traveling mud show, Howes' Great London Circus (an American show except for its name). He was paid the munificent salary of five dollars a month plus room and board. As a cage boy, he observed closely how Louis Roth, the famous trainer with whom he worked, handled the wild animals. While cleaning cages, feeding the carnivores and carrying out other duties, he learned as much as he could about the habits of the animals. Within two years his enthusiasm, general understanding of animal behavior and apparent capability led to his being given his own act with five performing bears.

The novice trainer learned quite by accident that an imposing 400-pound, 6-foot bear standing on his short hind legs could do a

UNITED PRESS INTERNATIONAL

somersault. A bruin had clutched Beatty during one of his early training sessions. Beatty delivered a strong punch to the animal's nose and it went into a complete backward turnover. A somersaulting stunt was thus added to the standard repertoire of performing bears by using a tap on the animal's face as a cue. Since bears were easier to teach than big cats, Beatty also taught the shaggy-haired mammals to march around in a circle and to ride bicycles.

From the early 1920's Beatty traveled with various companies continuing his apprenticeship. His big chance came after he had joined the Hagenback-Wallace Show. When the circus trainer developed a heart attack, Beatty was called upon to take over. Then, still in his twenties, Beatty was the youngest wild animal trainer in the country.

53

The years spent with the various circus companies revealed to Beatty that animals must be trained properly from the beginning and that one of the cardinal rules was to let the beast know who was master. Though he had only a few years of experience, Beatty displayed a certain authority which made the ferocious animals respond to his command. He learned that a bloodthirsty tiger (or "tager" as he called them), though treacherous, is confused and afraid of what he cannot understand. Beatty took advantage of the fact that animals generally back away when chair legs are directed toward them. Similarly, a long pole shoved through the bars could offer protection for the trainer. A keen sense of timing, an important element in the handling of these animals, contributed to his success.

Beatty was still working for the Hagenback-Wallace Show in 1926 when he distinguished himself by assembling forty male and female lions and tigers in one cage at the same time— a spectacle reminiscent of the great Colosseum pageants. The youthful trainer began to develop his own personal style in handling the big cats. Over the years he perfected a highly sophisticated technique, carrying a metal-reinforced chair, a revolver which fired only blanks, and a whip used only for the attention-getting snap. Other theatrics were employed to good advantage by the trainer to make the act even more sensational. For his performances and public appearances Beatty dressed like an African hunter of Hollywood movies — shiny boots, flaring white breeches and pith helmet. A "stare-down" was added for the benefit of audiences who breathlessly watched man pitted against wild beast in visual confrontation.

In 1934, Clyde Beatty (pronounced Bay-tee by the trainer, but Bee-tee by circus people) left the Hagenback-Wallace Show to form a company called the Cole Brothers & Clyde Beatty Circus. During the late 1930's and early 1940's, the Beatty show enjoyed tremendous popularity and success. By the mid-1940's several mergers and changes of command had taken place. In 1946 Beatty joined the Russell Brothers Pan-Pacific Circus in California, but the next season returned to operating his own company known as the Clyde Beatty Circus.

After World War II, the company made unprecedented tours of the western part of the United States and Canada. The number of railroad cars used to transport animals, performers and equipment made the Clyde Beatty Circus the largest railroad-borne circus other than that of the Ringling Brothers. The circus industry, however, went into a slump in the late 1950's because of such factors as rising costs, labor problems and difficulties in obtaining show lots. The Clyde Beatty Circus transferred its rolling stock and baggage from railroad cars to trucks, where it was not bound to the uncertainties of train schedules, using this mode of transportation for the next several years.

Beatty succeeded in enlisting the talents of many popular performers of the center ring in his own circus show. But it was the wild animal acts depicted on vivid and colorful posters for which the show was primarily noted. He continued to present a large number of "jungle cats" together in one cage, feeling that groups of mixed animals, though more dangerous, made a more exciting show. Also, in the event of a melee among the animals, it would distract their attention from the man in the cage, for lions and tigers hate each other more than they hate man. Jungle cats were considered by Beatty to be smarter than those born in captivity. He claimed that the latter were more difficult to handle and generally spoiled. From his observations, Beatty learned that the wild felines did more damage with their teeth than with their claws—the converse of what was popularly believed.

54

COLE BROS CIRCUS

CLYDE BEATTY
GREATEST WILD ANIMAL TRAINER OF ALL TIME

Clyde Beatty "staring down"
animals during his act. Beatty
played up confrontation of man and beast.

Beatty also noted that it was good for animals to use their teeth and grind up a few bones along with their meals of raw meat. It seemed to make them happier. In his numerous books on the training of jungle cats, he dispelled the myth that animals had to be fed before each performance so that they would be less inclined to make a meal of the trainer. Beatty explained that if animals were fed then it would only make them sleepy, and therefore he insisted that they be fed after each performance.

Beatty's act with all its fury and dramatic flourishes of blanks being fired and whip cracking to the accompaniment of fast tempo music was in contrast to the European wild animal act. European trainers put on a tableau as opposed to "en férocité" displays. They cue their animals by unobtrusive signals of hands and arms. The Beatty kind of act probably adds an extra element of risk.

Lions can be trained to jump through a fiery hoop, and tigers to leap through the air to another pedestal, but they can never really be tamed. The trainer must always be on guard against their primitive instinct. If a big cat gets out of control a trainer must never turn his back on the animal. Beatty wrote in one of his books that the man in the cage should always work back so that he is nearest the door and never let the animal get between him and that door.

The danger of wild animal acts is borne out by the numerous brushes with death that Beatty and other trainers have suffered in the cage. Bites, mauling and clawing hospitalized Beatty many times after his forays in the arena. He was once unconscious for twelve days after a lion seized him and dragged him around the perimeter of the ring. The animal dropped Beatty only after ammonia fumes sprayed into the cage blinded the animal temporarily.

Clyde Beatty was short, wiry and nimblefooted. He had curly hair, eyes that looked through you rather than at you, flaring nostrils and a gravelly voice. In some ways he resembled the animals that he confronted daily. It was generally thought unwise to visit the trainer after a knife-edged performance with the big cats. Although Beatty demonstrated great confidence and authority in the cage, the daily encounter was still a nerveracking experience and left him tense.

The feats of this almost legendary hero of the steel arena from the early 1920's through the mid-1960's added another dimension to the development of circus entertainment. In his later years Beatty appeared in films, on radio and television. He also found time to record his observations and experiences in several books. On July 19, 1965, cancer claimed the life of one of the world's greatest animal trainers.

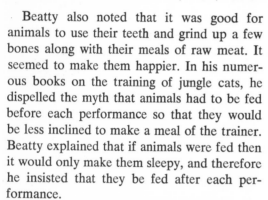

12
May Wirth

Queen of the Bareback Riders

I was only a five-foot little girl and my horse was sixteen and a half hands high.... When I did the "feet jump" I counted off a certain number of paces as the horse galloped around the ring. Then I jumped up onto his back and off again to the ground ....Sometimes I finished off the act by jumping with baskets tied to my feet.*

This unusual stunt was recalled during a recent interview of the woman who performed it in the early years of this century.

Gracious and still sprightly, May Wirth who is presently retired and living in Sarasota, Florida, has a sharp memory for details of the many tricks she did on horseback during her circus career. She modestly relates this in a

*Personal interview with May Wirth.

gentle voice with a trace of an Australian accent. Her scrapbook of pictorial memories brings back to life her extraordinary talents as "Queen of the Bareback Riders" during the twenty-six years she appeared in this country.

May Wirth, born in Queensland, Australia, came from a family of riders and other circus entertainers. The Wirth Brothers Circus, operated by her uncles, was a prestigious circus troupe in Australia. May Wirth's mother was ring-mistress, and she started training May and her sister in the art of bareback riding at an early age. Before May was in her teens she was already an accomplished equestrienne appearing with the Wirth circus. A fellow performer at that time was the famed rope-twirling American humorist, Will Rogers, who entertained audiences "down under" as well as in

PHOTO COURTESY OF SAN ANTONIO PUBLIC LIBRARY, HERTZBERG COLLECTION.
USED WITH PERMISSION OF RINGLING BROS.—BARNUM & BAILEY COMBINED SHOWS, INC.

other parts of the world.

In 1912, when May Wirth was sixteen years old, John Ringling brought her to this country to appear at Madison Square Garden. When the two great circuses, Barnum and Bailey and Ringling Brothers merged in 1919, May Wirth was one of the featured stars, and the center ring was reserved for her performance. Posters displayed during the twenties proclaimed May Wirth "The Greatest Bareback Rider That Ever Lived." This accolade is supported by those who remember her breathtaking acrobatics and delicate technique on horseback.

In addition to her mother's early tutelage in riding when she was a little girl, Miss Wirth studied in the United States with the well-known rider, Orrin Davenport. Mr. Davenport, who later directed Shrine circuses, considered May Wirth one of the "finest artists" whose style was unmatched by any other. She was often thought of as a "performer's performer" because of her adroit mastery of acrobatics and bareback riding. Although she could do a forward somersault effortlessly on horseback, it was Mr. Davenport who taught her to do the backward somersault. May Wirth soon exceeded this feat by introducing the back-backward somersault! The petite equestrienne would take off while standing with her back to the horse's head. By throwing her body over and making a half twist she would come out of the turn facing forward while the rosinback continued galloping around the ring. She was the only woman til that time to have attempted this stunt, and she executed this as gracefully as a ballerina, scarcely touching the horse's back as she gyrated. She was also quite skilled at somersaulting from one moving horse to another.

On one visit to her homeland, May Wirth learned the "flip-flap" routine which an Australian rider, John Cooke, taught her, and she added it to her repertoire of bareback riding accomplishments. While she was standing on the back of a horse galloping furiously around the ring she would flip to her hands then back again to her feet, repeating this several times.

When she did her famous "feet jump" stunt she never used a jumping board but depended solely on her "lift"— catapulting her body onto the back of the running horse. "But first I had to run like the dickens to catch up to him," she laughingly recalled. This was truly a remarkable stunt when one considers the size of the performer, the height of the horse and the precision demanded of her to be at the right spot at the right moment. She later wore market baskets on her feet, making the trick a more fearful challenge. Few persons possessed the coordination and stamina necessary for this act. Months of training were required for an appearance which lasted less than ten minutes on the program.

May Wirth learned early in her career that when one falls on one's back, it is best to stiffen the body so that one can bounce right back on one's feet. During the twenty-six years that she appeared in the center ring, she had a few minor scuffs to her "rider's left leg" but only one serious accident which occurred in Brooklyn, New York, around 1913. She was performing in a cowgirl sequence in which she lay on the horse's back with one foot placed precariously in a rope-loop stirrup. The horse was momentarily distracted by something a worker dropped nearby and shied. May Wirth slipped to the ground with her foot still in the stirrup. She was dragged around for five full circuits while her head repeatedly struck the ring-curb like a wrecking ball. She was knocked out completely and suffered a concussion. While she was recuperating in her hotel room Mr. John Ringling visited her every day. With the indomitable spirit which is characteristic of circus heroes and heroines, she returned to the arena after her recovery.

May Wirth performed
"impossible" tricks on horseback
with grace and precision.

May Wirth appeared with the Ringling Brothers and Barnum & Bailey Circus from 1916 to 1929, which included the era of the Golden Twenties. During the winter months she demonstrated her equestrian talents in vaudeville shows on the Keith and Orpheum circuits. When she toured abroad audiences which included royalty frequently attended her performances. Some of the royal persons who witnessed her daring feats on horseback were King Edward VII and Queen Alexandra. While in America, presidents Harding and Wilson were among those who watched her sensational act. When President Wilson, who always enjoyed the circus, became crippled by a stroke, he attended one of the shows at a Washington theater in a wheelchair which was pushed up a special runway.

After 1929, the year she left the Ringling Brothers Circus, May Wirth continued her active career as a bareback rider, playing longer engagements instead of one night stands. During this period she appeared in variety shows and fairs. She retired in 1938 at the peak of her career.

After living for a while in New England, the "Greatest Bareback Rider" settled in Sarasota, Florida, where she could be among the friends she had known during her circus years. Her husband, who was a producer and booking agent for circus shows, is deceased. Today one of her constant companions is her frisky dog "Cooe" named after the Australian bushman's call for help.

Among the many honors bestowed upon this beautiful woman is a special plaque bearing a gold horse, presented to her recently by the "Circus Folks Club" in Sarasota as part of their recognition of circus celebrities from former years.

Petite May Wirth, whose merry brown eyes twinkle as she relives her many years in the dazzling center ring, enjoys sharing her memories with people who drop by. In her living room is a petit point stitchery created by her sister, which shows a young, attractive, smiling girl with a pink bow in her hair posing next to her favorite horse—a simple reminder of the many years this woman spent as "Queen of the Bareback Riders."

13
Merle Evans

Maestro of the Circus World

CIRCUS WORLD MUSEUM, BARABOO, WISCONSIN

Merle Evans once summed up his sixty years as a bandmaster by calling himself, "just a Kansas boy who likes to blow a cornit." With these words the famous and enduring bandmaster Merle Evans in understated simplicity describes his sixty years on the bandstand. Almost fifty of those years were spent with the Ringling Brothers Circus. For nearly twenty-five thousand performances the "Toscanini of the Big Top" provided the musical timing essential to the presentation of each act.

He directed with his left hand and held "the cornit"— as he refers to the cornet in his twangy mid-Western voice—in his right hand. In this way he cued more than 200 musical changes for each complete show twice daily, rhythmically pacing the excitement of every act. After more than four million cues the man, whose name comes to mind whenever circus band music is mentioned, continues to be active at conducting and blowing his cornet.

As a youngster, Kansas-born Merle Evans worked at a variety of jobs, delivering papers, shining shoes and cleaning up at a greenhouse among other things. When he was ten years old, he joined a newly formed band in his home town, Columbus, Kansas. Even at this early age, his ability to produce "the strongest sound in the state" on his new John Slater cornet made it necessary for him to go off to empty barns and fields where he could practice to his heart's content — away from the sensitive ears of his family and friends. His early experience with the town band eventually determined his life's work. However, he held scores of jobs before 1919 when he joined the Ringling Brothers Circus as band director.

The larger world outside of Columbus beckoned, and at fifteen he took a job with a traveling show called the S. W. Brundage Carnival. In addition to playing the cornet, Merle was shortly informed by the owner that he was responsible for assembling and dismantling the carrousel. After one season with the carnival, Evans left and for a brief period added his unique cornet power to the strains of a Salvation Army band. He then worked at several other odd jobs, including racking balls in a Salina poolroom, until learning of a position available in a showboat band. He signed on the *Cotton Blossom* traveling down the Mississippi, putting on performances at the river towns along the way. During the day Merle Evans spent his time on the theater-barge practicing on his cornet and fishing; in the evenings on the foredeck he blared out favorite melodies in the band.

After a season with the showboat the young cornetist, in search of a new adventure, teamed up with a friend and fellow musician, "Doc" Pullen, to form a medicine show. The musical selections provided by Pullen and Evans were a prelude to a lengthy sales pitch on the merits of a concoction which supposedly could cure anything from leprosy to cretinism. After a short time with the medicine show, Merle Evans resumed his wanderings through the Midwest, working with various theatrical and musical groups.

In the fall of 1913 he joined a town band in Campbell, Missouri. Evans recalls that he once surprised a group of Holy Rollers who were holding a riverside tent meeting in that town. He dressed as the angel Gabriel and blew a blast on his cornet which could be heard "all over the Midwest," just as the fervor of the religious gathering was approaching its height near midnight. When the members of this group heard the explosive burst of sound, they were sure that the world was coming to an end and fled in every direction.

In 1916 Merle Evans appeared in a Wild West show with William F. Cody, one year before his death. Evans added to his list of unusual employments an appearance with a theatrical show, a minstrel show and a job as a portable phonograph salesman.

Merle Evans once during these years attended a performance of the Ringling Brothers Circus when it played in Sioux City, Iowa. Upon seeing the magnificent show and particularly the bandwagon and its musicians, he recognized that this was what he really wanted to do. He immediately applied to the manager for a job with the show. In 1919 the hayseed musician was informed by a telegram from Charles Ringling that he was hired. Evans was asked to report for work "at your earliest convenience." Thus began Evans' association with the Greatest Show on Earth, from 1919 to his retirement in 1969. Evans missed few performances except those during a musicians' strike in 1942 and a four-year stint with other shows from 1956 to 1960.

This incredible bandmaster had been with the Ringling Brothers Circus from the era of the Golden Twenties, when such stellar performers as Leitzel, Codona, and May Wirth appeared, through the years with the Concellos, the Wallendas, the Cristianis and the Loyal-Repenskis. He has survived the "blowdowns" of the tent in severe windstorms, train wrecks and a runaway bandwagon with ten horses speeding down a Boston street in 1919. Evans has also seen the circus change from a traveling tent show to performances in permanent arenas.

During the non-circus months Merle Evans traveled with Fred Bradna's Indoor Circus or staged his own tours in the North. For three seasons, Evans led the band at the Mills Brothers Winter Circus in London where talented entertainers from all over Europe and America appeared.

When Merle Evans started with the Ringling Brothers Circus, the band consisted of thirty-six musicians. Charles Ringling, a devotée of music, liked the band to have a full and rich sound. In the early years Evans often played cornet-baritone duets with Charles Ringling in the circus owner's private railroad car. Down through the years the number of musicians had been reduced to twenty-five members who tried to maintain the same volume of sound from the bandstand. When violins were added to the circus band in the late 1950's during Evans' absence, protests were voiced by circus band purists. As musical performance styles have changed, so too has the structure of the band.

During his almost half century of conducting and playing his cornet with the Greatest Show on Earth, Evans had to find melodies

suitable for acts ranging from frilly-skirted, pirouetting elephants to flyers' daring midair triple somersaults. In order to organize these compositions Evans had to be thoroughly familiar with the entire program, including the staging and choreography as well as other production problems. After he observed how the acts were blocked in and learned their sequence, it was his task to adapt appropriate musical arrangements to fit them. At each performance excerpts from selections in the broad musical library of waltzes, sambas, rumbas, marches, galops, fanfares and show tunes were matched to the specific action in the center ring.

Merle Evans stood with his back to the band, signaling them when to "segue," or quickly change to another tune without stopping, while playing the cornet with his right hand. Evans' brilliant musicianship and sensitive awareness of each action enabled him to conduct the many switchovers necessary to a smooth production.

Evans learned early in his circus experience that when wild animals were performing they were unpredictable and that it was best to watch the trainer. But when dancing horses cavorted, he had to follow their steps closely so that the tempo of the music would fit precisely. By observing each movement of every performer and tanbark act, Evans and his group of skilled musicians provided the "heartbeat" of the circus — the exciting band music. They played appropriate tunes to accompany the roar of the Bengal tigers, bicycling bears, daredevil wire-walkers, the twirling "iron-jaw" ladies, trotting horses and the merry antics of the clowns spilling out into the circus arena.

Another amazing feat which Merle Evans mastered was the ability to blow high C on his cornet while simultaneously eating popcorn—a favorite food during his early Big-Top days. "I've never met a person or a bag of pop-corn I didn't like" is a statement characteristic of his down-home humor which earned him the title of "Will Rogers with a horn." The cheery, always smiling bandmaster has made numerous friends all over the world. His remarkable knack of remembering names is phenomenal.

The music which Evans played for the Ringling Brothers Circus included the once popular high-speed galops used for some entrances and exits. The "Fire Jump" galop was one of the many which he himself composed. The fanfares are perhaps best known for their magnificent, ear-shattering flourishes. Among the many other musical selections which Evans composed was a melody called "Fredella" written for Fred and Ella Bradna, the famous ringmaster and his equestrienne wife who served with Evans during his long tenure with the Ringling Circus. A tune which he dedicated to that devoted group of circus aficionados, The Circus Fans of America, is another band favorite. There were also some standby melodies used only in the event that one of the performers in the center ring had a mishap. These reassuring musical signals meant, "It's all right, start over again."

Perhaps the most tragic number Evans ever had to play was the traditional song of disaster — Sousa's "Stars and Stripes Forever" — during the tragic fire in Hartford, Connecticut, in 1944. Evans was among the first to spot the

Left: Early circus band
headed by Merle Evans.

Right: Cornet used by Evans.

flames as they raced along the tent rope. He immediately gave the signal and the band swung into the warning music, alerting the roustabouts and the performers.

The music in circuses today is very different from that which was formerly played. Nowadays, show tunes are the staple of the bands, forming background music similar to that of ice shows. Galops, "smears" and other old styles are rarely played anymore.

Mr. Evans has a fascinating photographic memory which serves him as a personal musical filing cabinet. Thousands of musical selections of various tempos, styles and rhythms are in this storehouse. With admirable facility he is able to retrieve any musical phrase for an accompaniment at a moment's notice.

In 1930 Merle Evans and his band were the first to make a phonograph record of circus music, and in the early 1940's they were the first to record a complete album of circus selections. His musicians, the "Windjammers," were among the early groups who appeared regularly on network radio.

The first time Evans was away from the bandstand was in 1942. A salary dispute between the musicians' union and the circus resulted in a strike. Torn by strong loyalties to his men as well as to the circus owners, Evans temporarily left his post, and the music for the program was provided by phonograph records. During the several months that Evans was away, he secured a job as band director on the faculty of Hardin-Simmons University in Abilene, Texas. His brief tenure at the school is fondly recalled by the many and lasting friends he made while conducting there.

Another landmark in the career of the illustrious bandmaster from Kansas is the tour which the circus made to the Soviet Union in the mid-1960's, sponsored by a governmental exchange program. He taught the circus musicians of that country some of the familiar American melodies and how to compose or "set up" music specifically for the circus. During this journey to Russia the company learned some interesting statistics— for example there were eighty performing circus companies and thirty single-ring buildings which housed shows in the U.S.S.R.

Since leaving the Ringling Brothers Circus in 1969, Evans has not been idle. He is driven by the energy which has been part of him since his early days in Columbus, Kansas. He still maintains his roots in his home town by being a member of the Board of Directors of the Columbus State Bank. Tall, gray-haired, grandfatherly-looking, Merle Evans is spry and vigorous. He walks with the quick gait of a young man in a hurry. A ready smile and easy manner accompany his conversations which are frequently peppered with humorous stories recalled from his long experience with the circus. When he is not appearing "on dates" across the United States as guest conductor and cornet player with bands, he lives in Sarasota, Florida, with his charming wife, Nena, in a bright, comfortable home whose walls are covered with awards.

Nena, whom he married in 1950, was formerly a secretary for John Ringling North and Henry Ringling North as well as other top-ranking circus officials. In addition to these executive duties Mrs. Evans also handled the intricate paper work and payroll for the vast operations. She speaks with grace and modesty as she tells of mornings she was driven by a chauffeured limousine from her house to the Ringling offices.

When Merle Evans makes his current appearances as guest conductor at band concerts, the smiling, waving bandmaster comes on stage in his familiar red uniform with gold trim. At these times he is greeted by prolonged standing ovations of senior citizens and young people alike who have come to hear and see the world's most famous living bandmaster.

63

14
The Flying Concellos

Daring Team On the Flying Trapeze

A trapeze artist was once asked the secret of doing a triple somersault from a swinging bar high above the audience. His answer was simply, "Keep turning and don't pause between somersaults!"

The history of the flying trapeze, the first innovation in many centuries of acrobatics and tumbling, originated in a small gymnasium in the Toulouse section of France in the early nineteenth century. A young French aerialist, Jules Léotard (for whom the dancing and acrobatic costume is named), fastened a bar between two ropes which hung like a swing from the ceiling of his father's gym, thus creating the flying trapeze as we know it today. Before that time only stationary bars were used by acrobats. After young Léotard made his debut on the flying trapeze at the Cirque Napoléon in the early 1800's, trapeze flying became so popular that many performers eagerly took to swinging high above the heads of the spectators. The art of "flying" developed over many years, but not until the time of Codona and Concello did it reach the sophistication which ultimately resulted in the spectacular mid-air triple somersault.

Executing three complete revolutions of one's body in the highest reaches of the arena is a feat which has been performed by only a few intrepid aerialists. Alfredo Codona began in 1920 to perform this spine-chilling trick, continuing to do so for over ten years. This handsome flyer became famous for the style and form which characterized his performances. The Concellos as a flying team were unique in that each of them could execute the triple on the same program. Arthur and Antoinette Concello displayed the ease of swooping birds in their aerial artistry. Their apparent weightlessness as they performed the awesome triple amazed audiences for many years. This unusual stunt is one of the most formidable to execute. After climbing the rope ladder to the pedestal, the aerialist must take several swings back and forth high above the ring to develop a speed of over sixty miles an hour in order to gain the momentum necessary to roll forward three times and come out of the third somersault into the waiting hands of the catcher.

In the 1930's and early 1940's, while at the height of their fame, the short and energetic Arthur (Art) Concello not only perfected this stunt but also could do two backward somersaults with a half twist as well as a double horizontal pirouette and other extraordinary feats. These tricks were done twice daily in the brief six minutes of their act. Although Concello's performance was incomparable, those who worked with him observed that he performed with a casual indifference amounting to boredom. He was so preoccupied with thoughts other than flying that he once climbed up to the high platform still wearing his street shoes. More than once he almost launched one of his daring leaps with his perennial cigar still in his mouth. His ambitious mind was frequently on the front office, trying to figure out ways to make the circus operation more efficient. When questioned recently about his career as the world's most famous trapeze artist, he shrugged it off with the simple statement, "It was just a matter of making a living."

Neither Art nor Antoinette Concello was born into a circus family as is often the case with performers. Art was born Arthur Vas Concello of Portuguese parentage in Spokane, Washington, where the elder Concello worked for the railroad. Arthur was three years old when the family moved to Bloomington, Illinois. When Art was ten years old he visited the Bloomington "Y" and watched the physical education instructor give trapeze demonstrations. Young Concello was so impressed by what he saw that he soon took lessons in trapeze flying, responding like a swallow to the sky.

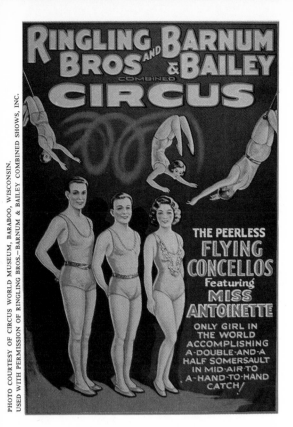

The Flying Concellos
became the most celebrated aerial team
after they joined the Big Top.

At age sixteen, Concello decided that he had had enough formal education and joined the "Flying Wards," one of the featured attractions of the Hagenbeck-Wallace Circus in Bloomington. Their son Eddie Ward, Jr., later became a Concello catcher. Though Concello was frequently absent or late to rehearsals, he managed to dazzle fellow performers by his superb artistry in the air. Ideas for improving the trapeze rigging as well as other innovations were percolating in his mind even at this early date.

Concello met his first wife while working with the Hagenbeck-Wallace Circus. The former Antoinette Comeau was startling audiences at the Sells-Floto Circus, also based in Bloomington, with the difficult "iron-jaw" trick in which she twirled at the end of a rope while hanging by her teeth. This tiny, pert woman was one of six children born in Burlington, Vermont, of French-Canadian and English extraction. She had no idea that she would become a circus performer when she graduated from a convent school at age fourteen. She was about to enter college on a scholarship when her sister and brother-in-law who worked with the Sells-Floto Circus asked

her to join them. Under the tutelage of the Wards Antoinette learned to become a catcher.

Concello left the Hagenbeck-Wallace show and came to the Sells-Floto Circus to work with the Wards. He and Antoinette were married and made their debut as a team in 1929. A year later, after Ringling had bought the American Circus Corporation which owned these two companies, the Concellos became members of The Big Show. Their act was performed in one of the side rings of the giant three-ring arena. The center ring was retained for the superlative flying of Alfredo Codona. In 1933, while attempting the triple somersault, Codona injured his shoulder and was forced to give up flying. Art and Antoinette were asked to move over into the middle ring. In this spotlighted position they went on to become the most celebrated aerial team that ever flew.

From 1933 on into the early forties, Concello started coaching other flyers. He began to operate his own school where he trained students in the tremendously complicated art of aerial soaring. When the aerialists had successfully completed their training, Concello booked units of these flyers into the Ringling circus as well as other circus companies all over the United States, England and Australia.

A flyer must, from the beginning of his training, learn how to fall properly and use the safety net judiciously; otherwise he can be badly injured. It is important when falling from a high swing onto the net to land on one's back, then bounce up and land secondly on one's feet. The net must be kept slightly loose to prevent rope burns which result if the net is too taut. For a time some European countries blacked out the nets to heighten the drama for the audience, but visiting American performers were disturbed by this since they could not accurately gauge its location. Grueling months of practice using a "mechanic"

Split-second timing is key to midair change in partners by the Flying Concellos.

— the leather safety harness which all trainees must use in practice — are essential before an aerialist is permitted to fly and spin on his own. But above all, split-second precision timing is most important.

Although Antoinette Concello was already proficient at many aerial stunts Arthur began grooming her for the triple somersault. One summer day in 1937 while in Detroit he felt that the time had come for Antoinette to do the triple. She later admitted she was so frightened she could hardly breathe. The petite aerialist responded brilliantly and, through her many achievements on the trapeze bar, became the undisputed "Queen of the Flying Trapeze."

Antoinette Concello was the only woman in the 1930's and 1940's to master the triple somersault. Her flying was so graceful that it was often called poetry in air. Following an injury to her shoulder, which is the bane of all circus flyers, Antoinette left the circus in 1943. After an absence of six years, during

which time a son was born to the Concellos, Antoinette resumed flying in 1949. She later retired from active trapeze work to take on her present role as aerial director of The Greatest Show on Earth.

Art Concello was always anxious to get into the management aspect of the circus, having studied and observed every phase of it from the time he joined as a performer. He was also aware that an aerialist has a limited career span. At the time he was asked to take over the post of general manager in 1943 and exchange his trapeze costume for a business suit, he was well-equipped to handle the complex job. Later, in 1947 when a shift in the Ringling family ownership dictated a change, Concello left The Big Show temporarily and went to the West Coast where he purchased the California-based Russell Brothers Circus. He left after several seasons and returned East to rejoin Ringling Brothers.

Upon his return, with his characteristic abundance of ambition and confidence, Con-

Below left: Antoinette and Arthur Concello.

Below right: Antoinette Concello
practicing flying before
Madison Square Garden opening in 1949.

cello introduced a series of innovations and inventions which were major contributions to the circus world. He tightened up operations thus improving the overall financial picture. His idea for more efficient, modern seating— the portable steel grandstand—was one of the most significant equipment changes in the history of the circus. In 1947 he perfected, patented and had manufactured mechanized wagons with built-in sections of folding seats. The system was used for the first time in the following year. Whereas previously it took many men four hours to set up the wooden grandstand and thousands of chairs, it became possible to do the same job in only forty-five minutes with fewer men. Steel safety stairways were a part of the system. Out of the fertile mind of the former aerialist also came the idea for aluminum side and quarter tent poles. Before the switch to permanent buildings and the elimination of menageries, he suggested that the Big Top be lengthened to include the animals, thereby doing away with separate tents for each.

In 1956 John Ringling North made the historic speech in which he stated that the tented circus was a thing of the past and that all future performances of the Ringling Brothers circus would be held in the permanent arenas of various cities. To accommodate the new indoor format Concello devised another first — a new type of tunnel car for transporting wagons containing equipment and animals. He also reorganized old productions and planned new ones. He even assisted the Ringling operation by lending money when financial crises arose.

Concello was in and out of the Ringling management during the fifties and sixties. He was also associated with the Clyde Beatty Circus on several occasions. The ex-flyer and executive genius left the world of the circus in 1968 to pursue other business and real estate interests. He is presently married to a British woman who was formerly a ballet dancer with the Ringling circus. They make their home in Sarasota, Florida. The man who "never cared much for flying" tends to minimize his own achievements over the years. Art's lively, colorful and outgoing personality has lost none of the spark which made him an adept performer and extremely successful circus manager — and he is still the same inveterate cigar smoker.

15
Famous Clowns

The Many Faces of Joey

The story is told that the original "Joey," master of the absurd, lay ill in bed, depressed and melancholic. His physician advised him to relax, go to the theater, "and make sure you see that fellow Grimaldi; he'll make you laugh and you'll feel much better." "But Doctor, I *am* Grimaldi," moaned the patient.

Joseph Grimaldi was an actor-clown popular with Drury Lane and Sadler's Wells audiences in London during the early 1800's. Though he was successful at making audiences roar with laughter, his own life was burdened by tragedies. His personal problems, however, were promptly forgotten as soon as he walked out onto the stage. Attired in his puffy-sleeved, baggy satin costume, standing with his knees together, toes pointing inward — he immediately evoked rollicking laughter. His face became contorted in a series of hilarious expressions as he performed various pantomime skits and sang witty songs. One classic number was "An Oyster Crossed in Love" where he sang a love song while gazing at an oyster on the half-shell. As he finished singing, he devoured the delicacy. Amusing people by exaggerating and mimicking their foibles was his forte. The fame of Joseph Grimaldi was so great that to this day a clown is called "Joey" in honor of this genius of comedy.

The history of clowns can be traced at least as far back as the times of ancient Greece and Rome. During the Middle Ages court jesters, wearing bell-adorned costumes, diverted kings from their problems and sometimes influenced royal decisions by their wit and amusing jokes. The traditional whiteface clown derives from the harlequin character of the commedia dell'arte which flourished in sixteenth-century Italy.

There are presently two fundamental types of clowns: the whiteface and the Auguste. The whiteface clown, stemming from the Middle Ages, has been traditional since that time. The whiteface makeup generally includes a red spot on each cheek, a red or black outline around the mouth, a large bulbous nose and pompom button decorations down the front of a full-cut costume.

The Auguste, or "clumsy fool," clown ostensibly originated in Germany in the 1860's when Tom Belling, a rider with the Renz Circus in Berlin, tried on the oversized pants of a stable boy. He was discovered by the ill-tempered owner of the show and, while trying to escape from him, inadvertently ran into the center ring. The audience accepted the merry chase and hilarious attempt to remove the clothing as part of the show and was convulsed by the awkward situation. The character of Auguste has remained a blundering stumblebum who, while trying to help others, is always getting into scrapes. His face may be white or pink with exaggerated features. A puzzled look on his face is heightened by greatly accentuating the makeup of his eyes. He generally wears a big nose and paints a wide grin around his mouth. His appearance is always untidy with baggy clothing and large flapping shoes, and he often carries a gadget designed to explode or ignite.

There are other kinds of clowns which are variants of the two basic types. One of these is the grotesque clown who wears the most bizarre or outlandish costume he can create. His face is generally white with large, overdone, red-painted lips, a big putty nose and bold splashes of color for tear marks and eyebrow lines. He wears a foolish hat, elongated shoes and may carry a small prop in his hand such as a tiny umbrella in contrast to his exaggerated costume.

The character clown is unmistakable; he usually dresses like a tramp. He has a grayish-black unshaven beard painted over a reddish face, and a white mouth, red nose and pathetic, sorrowful eyes. His clothes are too large and frequently tattered and torn, often

Midget car serves
as laugh-provoking prop for
clown, Lou Jacob.

with strips held together by safety pins. There is an air of total hopelessness about him—nothing in his act ever seems to turn out right as he strolls in bewilderment around the arena. Emmett Kelly is the most famous of present-day tramp clowns.

There are also walk-around and producing clowns who use either an animal or other prop as an integral part of their comic routines. Felix Adler was familiar to audiences for his walk-around act with a small pig. Perhaps the best-known producing clown is Lou Jacob, who has devised and built Lilliputian motorized vehicles into which he compresses his huge, lanky frame. A carpet clown is one who mingles with the audience and does his tricks while the acts change. Acrobatic, riding, midget, and lady clowns are among the others in the roster of laugh merchants.

P. T. Barnum once said that clowns were pegs on which to hang circuses. Their comic business helps to bridge the gaps between performing numbers on a circus program. A throng of noisy clowns may come bursting forth in a whirlwind entrance into the arena. This is called a "charivari" or "shivaree." The clowns quickly do their tricks, then disappear into the wings, or "clown alley," until the next break occurs. As a former clown with the Ringling circus sums it up, "We just get in and get out; we don't labor the point." The broad slapstick type of humor which takes place briefly while the next act is being prepared helps maintain the continuity and smooth flow of the performance.

Clown alley is the name given to the dressing room where all the clowns gather to put on their greasepaint and costumes. They are in and out of the arena so frequently that a specific place is necessary for changing and applying makeup. Countless jars of zinc oxide and glycerine, the base for all clown makeup, and tubes and jars of brilliant colors are lined up along the tables as well as gadgets, gimmicks and other accoutrements that the funnymen use in their trade.

The individual makeup and costumes of the clown are considered sacred in the circus world and no one may copy them. This is a generally accepted rule among members of the profession. Gags may be adapted, but makeup and other markings which are the special trademark of each clown may not be copied. While a gentleman's agreement dictates this, there are occasional imitators. In England, personal makeup designs are registered with the International Circus Clowns Club. For a time makeups of individual members were painted on eggshells and kept on display.

A Clown College is operated by a former clown, Bill Ballantine, at the winter quarters of the Ringling Bros. and Barnum & Bailey Circus. During the intensive six-week course, students learn pantomime, makeup, acrobatics and visual comedy. Those students who complete the course receive a diploma upon graduation, and some are awarded a contract to travel with the Ringling circus in its cross-country tour.

The first circus presented to American audiences by John Bill Ricketts featured a clown-trick rider named Tom Sully. In the early 1800's clowns told jokes and sang before the gathering crowds to stimulate interest for the shows. Joe Pentland, a well-known clown of that time, traveled with young P. T. Barnum in the early Aaron Turner Circus days. Perhaps the most famous of the talking and singing clowns was Dan Rice, whom we met earlier in this book.

As the tented circus grew and the intimate one-ring shows disappeared to make way for the giant three-ring extravaganzas — so did the singing and talking comics whose voices would not carry in the larger arenas. Pantomiming clowns again took the place of the vocal clowns.

69

Clown poster featuring Felix Adler
was issued in 1933.

Poodles Hanneford and Slivers Oakley were two clowns familiar to circus audiences in the early 1900's. Slivers was once honored by having a full five-minute solo act in Madison Square Garden devoted to his specialty — mimicking a one-man baseball team.

Felix Adler

The King of the Clowns in the earlier part of this century was a comic performer who made audiences laugh by his uproarious antics with a little pig. Felix Adler, who was born in Clinton, Iowa, ran away from home when he was twelve years old to join the Ringling Brothers Circus. His father later agreed that he might stay with the circus if he promised faithfully to attend classes during the school year and to work with the circus only in the summer time until he graduated. While working at his first job of carrying water for the horses and elephants, young Adler became fascinated by the clowns. He observed closely the mannerisms, costumes and techniques of their individual styles. The day he graduated from high school, he wrote Charles Ringling to ask for a permanent job. As a result he was hired as a clown.

During his career Adler trained more than five hundred piglets for his act. As each piglet became too large for the act, the clown would donate it to a farmer or any interested person along the circus route. Adler would then start the training of a new baby pig. The best-remembered routine of this famous walk-around clown was the one in which he trained the pig to climb up the steps of a slide board, then scoot down the other side. The animal's reward was a drink from a baby bottle.

"My gags are not elaborate — but they're sure-fire and they just seem to belong to me," said Adler in an interview in 1960. "In the old days the clown was the spectacle himself; today he has to fight every minute to get attention in the midst of the three-ring, five-level jamboree."

When asked the secret of his success with his routines, Adler replied, "The simpler the trick the better, so long as it contains an element of surprise." Adler knew that the same "simple" gags evoked laughter year after year. For five decades the clown with the perpetual grin and wearing a spotted costume tickled audiences at the Ringling Bros. and Barnum & Bailey Circus.

Known as the White House Clown for his many appearances before presidents Coolidge, Harding and F.D. Roosevelt, Adler also distinguished himself by being the first clown to appear on a television program in 1932. He died in 1960.

70

Otto Griebling

When Otto Griebling, son of a tailor, left his native Germany at the age of fifteen on his way to America, the ship he boarded went instead to Japan! He worked his way back to Germany and started his journey to America all over again. An ad in a newspaper which read "Wanted — circus bareback rider" caught his eye shortly after his arrival. The young boy responded to the ad and was hired to work as an apprentice rider in a small circus. However, the job was a short-lived one. The young rider, sent by the owner into town, left the troupe and decided to become a farm boy instead. When the circus returned to the same town two years later, young Griebling realized he had had enough of farm life. He asked for and was given his old job back. ". . . And I've been with circuses ever since."

Griebling spent ten years with the company as a horseback rider before he thought he might try clowning. His success at his new job was instantaneous, and the sorrowful-comical tramp characterization he created has remained popular since that time. Til recently he continued to be one of the headliners in the Greatest Show on Earth.

Griebling invented and developed many of his own gags. In one of his familiar routines he carried around an enormous block of ice, trying to find a taker. As he continued to look for someone to relieve him of the large, drippy armful, the block got smaller and smaller and finally melted away, much to the chagrin of the bewildered clown. He wore the same lonely expression of rejection as he sat knitting an endless, red, moth-eaten sweater among a bevy of beautiful girls.

As a producing clown Griebling is credited with one of the classic automobile and clown production numbers. He asked the Studebaker car company to produce a car into which twenty-six people could fit. They said it couldn't be done. Otto then explained to the perplexed engineers how it could be accom-

CIRCUS WORLD MUSEUM, BARABOO, WISCONSIN

plished. Soon circus audiences were laughing at the sight of one passenger after another, in almost infinite numbers, emerging from a small sedan. The last figure to emerge, after an appropriate pause, was not just another clown but one with an extra large prop.

The small, roundish figure of the tramp clown was also recognized as he attempted to kick another performer, but it was the sad little tramp character himself who usually fell down. Griebling's many years of experience as a horseback rider prepared him for the many pratfalls he took during his lifetime.

Emmett Kelly, a contemporary of Griebling and an illustrious performer in his own right, recalls that Otto was also a superb actor. The two performed a construction skit together. They would come out with lumber, saw and

71

blueprints, and with these implements they were going to rebuild and change the world. "Otto could look at you and know exactly what you were thinking. He could convey feeling and emotion and catch it in the other person," Kelly recently reminisced.

Griebling himself attributed his success at the business of being funny to being able to "understand human nature." Up to his recent death at seventy-five, he performed his famous pantomine making people laugh — an ability which he described as a "gift of God."

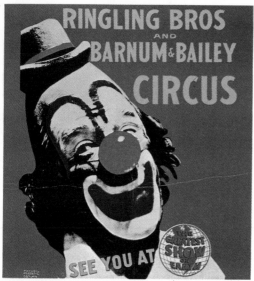

Lou Jacob

The broadly grinning white-faced clown with the funny little hat atop his long head symbolizes the circus to millions, for this is the celebrated clown whose face appears on the Ringlings' billboard posters!

Born in Wesermünde, Germany, Lou Jacob, who is also known as Lou Jacobs, studied acrobatics, balancing and body contortion as a young boy. He started his pro-

fessional career as a double contortionist with a partner who acted as a straight man. After coming to the United States in 1923, he toured fairs and appeared with vaudeville shows across the country. He also spent a year with the Morris and Morris Circus. It was while he starred with this company that he came to the attention of the Ringling brothers in 1925, and he has been with "The Big One" ever since. He is also a "professor" at the Ringling College of Clowns in Venice, Florida, where he helps train students who aspire to become circus funnymen.

Jacob has thought up hundreds of hilarious gags and props guaranteed to delight everyone from eight to eighty as soon as he enters the Big Top. Circus audiences can generally identify the familiar figure of Lou Jacob when a noisy miniature car, not much larger than a breadbasket, comes sputtering into the ring, and a tall, lanky clown steps out. This extraordinary feat is possible only because of his many years spent as a contortionist and acrobat. With his exceedingly inventive mind, Jacob has devised numerous other mechanical contrivances into which he eases his big, strapping frame. In addition to the minuscule auto, this producing clown has motorized a baby carriage and a bathtub. Another popular sight gag for which Jacob is known is the live dachshund tucked into a giant hot dog roll which he carries about the arena with him. Lou Jacob admits that he must have been "born with a funny bone in his body" in order to have produced laughter for as long as he has.

In 1953 he married Jean Rockwell, who was a circus performer until a fall injured her back several years ago. The couple have two daughters, Lou Ann and Dolly Jean. Lou Ann appears as one of the attractive show girls with the Ringling Brothers and Barnum & Bailey Circus on the same program as her famous and proud father.

Emmett Kelly

Life is one long frustration according to Willie. He is in his creator's words

a sad and ragged little guy who is very serious about everything he attempts — no matter how futile or how foolish it appears to be . . . . but there is always present that forlorn spark of hope glimmering in his soul that makes him keep on trying.*

A vagabond clown with a turned-down expression wearing a battered derby, bedraggled clothing and floppy shoes enters the ring. He is carrying a straggly broom. He starts to sweep away the pool of light made by an overhead spot. Diligently he sweeps the light into a dustpan as it gradually becomes smaller and smaller. Just as he thinks he has it finally collected in the pan he starts to walk away only to discover that it is still dogging him, becoming larger and larger, and he has to start all over again.

When "Weary Willie" the tramp clown lights a little fire and tries to warm his hands our hearts go out to him. When Willie blows up a balloon to its fullest capacity only to have it suddenly burst in his face he attempts to bury it in a small cemetery. This poignant bit he contrived after observing children at play. These vignettes of the sad-faced clown, who never speaks and for whom nothing ever turns out right as he wanders around the arena, make us simultaneously laugh and sympathize with him. There is no slapstick in this clown's performance, only the rare ability to elicit humor and pathos.

As a young boy, Emmett Kelly visited a circus in his home town of Sedan, Kansas, where his father worked as a section foreman for the Missouri-Pacific Railroad. The family later moved to Texas County in southwest Missouri where the elder Kelly bought a farm. While still in his teens, Emmett Kelly became interested in art, and his mother paid $25.00

*Emmett Kelly, *Clown*.

BROWN BROTHERS

for a correspondence course in cartooning for him. It was in 1920, when the youthful cartoonist was working for a silent film company in Kansas City where Walt Disney was also employed, that Emmett drew the hobo cartoon character which later took life and became the famed circus clown.

"Willie" was created by Emmett Kelly at the Adfilm Company for a bread advertisement. The young cartoonist drew the forlorn hobo with features similar to his own visage: a long face with sad-looking eyes, a dejected expression, mouth turned down and set in a squarish jaw. Kelly's own nose is thin and slightly upturned, but he gave the hobo a bulbous one instead. All of these features were adapted to the clown character which was later to become familiar to millions.

Emmett Kelly held a variety of jobs in those days which included work at a lumberyard, a creamery, a sign shop, and a dog and pony show. When the Ringling circus appeared in Kansas City, he didn't have seventy-five cents, the admission price of a ticket, and was too overwhelmed by the magnitude of the whole operation to ask for a job there. Kelly did find work, however, at

73

Doc Grubb's Western Show Property Exchange where he earned six cents apiece for painting carnival kewpie dolls. With three dollars that he managed to save he bought his first trapeze and rigging. At subsequent jobs with Zieger's United Shows and the Frisco Exhibition Shows he painted merry-go-rounds, sold sideshow tickets and, as he relates, "made myself otherwise generally useful." He also worked with a number of other circus companies as a trapeze artist and helped out as a whiteface clown.

Up to that time almost all of the clowns in American circuses wore whiteface makeup only. When Kelly thought he would present himself as Willie to circus audiences, the head clown where he worked did not approve. He believed that Kelly's comic portrayal in tattered clothing and unshaven face looked too dirty and that audiences would react unfavorably. The character of "Willie the tramp" was put aside, and Kelly continued to perform on the trapeze for the next nine years.

His partner at that time was his first wife, the former Eva Moore whom he had married in the early 1920's and who appeared with him in a double trapeze act until the birth of Emmett Kelly, Jr., the first of their two sons. For nearly a decade, while Kelly performed as a trapeze artist, he never forgot Willie. "I believed in him from the start," stated Kelly while reminiscing recently, and he appeared in this role whenever he could. Kelly recollects that in 1932 in Kokomo, Indiana, Willie and he were finally accepted.

As an additional source of income when not on the road with the circus, Kelly gave chalk-talks in nightclubs. Dressed in the rag-bag costume of the tramp, he would come out on stage with an easel, pad and chalk, then proceed to illustrate a short skit which he had written. With a few deft lines he also sketched a clump of trees which, turned upside down, resembled a prominent personality.

After working with several circus companies where he perfected his comedy routines, he joined the Cole Brothers & Clyde Beatty Circus in 1937. When it opened at the New York Hippodrome, Kelly in his role as the sad-faced clown received highly favorable reviews in the newspapers. He was singled out by the critics for his unique pantomiming. Although this acclaim provided a secure niche in circus history, both Willie and his creator were to live through many problems. The sad experience of a divorce, the witnessing of a tragic fire which claimed so many lives and the disappointment of seeing Willie's copyrighted face and costume imitated by others—all of these feelings inevitably worked their way into the character of the sad hobo who became indistinguishable from Emmett Kelly.

After appearing with the Cole Brothers & Clyde Beatty Circus for several years, in 1942 Kelly joined "The Big One"— the three-ring extravaganza of the Ringling Brothers and Barnum & Bailey Circus. John Ringling North had seen Kelly in London at the Bertram Mills Olympia Circus.

Emmett Kelly was with the Ringling circus when the catastrophic fire occurred in Hartford, Connecticut, in 1944. He was putting on the finishing touches to his makeup and waiting for his cue when a circus worker rushed by clown alley and yelled "Fire!" — a word which is the all-time nightmare of the circus business. Kelly ran immediately to the center ring to assist wherever he could. He repeatedly shouted "Keep moving!" to the panic-stricken crowd, some of whom wanted to turn back to locate relatives they believed were inside. A picture of the tramp clown in his baggy shoes and carrying a bucket of water, which he happened to grab as he ran to the ring, was published all over the world. Ironically, the performance scheduled for that day was to have featured Willie as the theme

Sad-faced Willie, created by Emmett Kelly, is the classic hobo character.

for the grand spectacular production number — the first time in circus history that a clown would have been so honored.

Kelly's life has consisted of a varied and colorful succession of occupations both in and out of the circus. In the early 1940's he acted in several Broadway productions including an Olsen and Johnson comedy show and a play, "Please Keep Off The Grass."

When Kelly made his film debut in 1950 in "The Fat Man," he played the role of a villain who was a Pagliacci-type clown. However, Kelly insisted that his makeup for this role be different from that of his well-known character role of Willie. He didn't want any of the stigma to carry over into the innocent clown, Willie. Emmett Kelly was also featured in the award-winning movie, "The Greatest Show on Earth," in 1951.

Kelly stayed with the Ringling Brothers show for fourteen seasons. In 1956 he spent one season away from the circus. Baseball fans will remember him as the funny tramp clown who strolled about the field whenever the Brooklyn Dodgers played, picking up bits and pieces of paper and performing his other little pantomine acts which have always captivated audiences. Since 1957 he has worked with the Shrine Circus. Audiences never tire of watching the hopeless-looking hobo shuffling around, nibbling on a leaf from an old cabbage. They are charmed by his wistful expression lighting up an otherwise downcast face when he spots an attractive girl in the audience and focuses a soulful gaze upon her.

Emmett Kelly was the first clown in circus history to be allowed the privilege of remaining in the ring to act on his own while others were performing. Many featured acts would urge him to add his own comic touch to their appearances. For example, when Lucio Cristiani, a member of the famous equestrian family, was preparing to begin his act, Willie would place a rickety ladder against the horse,

climb up a few steps and begin to wipe off the horse's back with a little broom. Or when the Wallendas were wire walking precariously high above the tanbark, the helpful tramp clown would stand under them with a handkerchief prepared to catch them if they fell.

When Kelly does his magnificent pantomime skits, he improvises as he moves about. He has observed that all parts of the audience do not react in the same way. After he finds the section where he gets the best response, he generally concentrates his act around this area. Applause rarely influences his decision. Perhaps one of the clues to his success lies in the fact that so many people identify with the pathetic soul who, though constantly blocked by frustrations, tries so hard in his little gestures to please. Many people, in turn, try to make the sad clown laugh, but he has developed little tricks over the years that ward off the impulse to smile.

The world-famous master of pathos and pantomime presently lives in Sarasota, Florida, with his lovely, petite, blond-haired wife and their two pretty teen-age daughters. His wife is a former gymnast from Germany who appeared with the Ringling Brothers Circus as part of a tumbling team called "The Four Whirlwinds."

The walls of their comfortable home are covered with paintings of the most popular hobo clown who ever lived, many done by prominent artists. In his book-lined study, there are numerous awards, citations and photos. On his desk is a copy of *Who's Who*, in which he has been given as much space as many important politicians and scientists.

The clown who has made millions laugh but who rarely smiles even in his private life points to his most treasured photo with gentle warmth — it shows Willie leaning close to a group of blind children who are tweaking his bulbous nose.

16
The Wallendas

Danger On the High Wire

While thousands of people stared at the slightly built sixty-five-year-old man walking on a high wire more than 700 feet above the floor of Georgia's Tallulah Gorge, his wife, a former wire walker, turned her head away from the awesome sight. Too many aerial tragedies were still etched in her mind.

Karl Wallenda performed this extraordinary feat on a 997-foot-long cable barely more than an inch and a half in diameter, using only a slender pole to maintain balance and doing two headstands along the way. This danger-filled accomplishment, which occurred in July of 1970, is only one of many executed by the man who is the leader of the most daring high-wire troupe in circus history.

When asked why he continues his dangerous profession, attempting such things as the gorge walk and other hair-raising stunts, Karl Wallenda replied: "When I get something in mind, I never let loose. . .and I always want to satisfy the public. . ." The public does indeed find excitement in watching such acts, and there are performers who constantly risk their lives to thrill the spectators.

There are two types of funambulists (a term derived from the Latin meaning rope walker), whose art can be traced back to ancient Greece: 1. The slack-wire walker who cavorts on a loosened wire strung relatively low above the ground. The wire is made taut by the weight of the walker, and the arms alone are used for balance. 2. The taut high-wire or tightrope walker who uses a balancing pole to help maintain equilibrium. Performing on the high wire above all demands great physical courage.

By walking across Niagara Falls on a tightrope, the Frenchman, Blondin (Jean François Gravelet), reawakened interest in this ancient art. On June 30, 1859, Blondin made his way precariously over the falls on a single rope 1,100 feet long. He later repeated this dizzying walk with several variations: blindfolded, on stilts, carrying a man on his back, and pushing a wheelbarrow.

During the early part of this century several talented rope performers were featured on the Ringling Brothers circus program. Bird Millman was the first American female to perform on the slack wire. This petite artist acquired her name because of the tiny, birdlike steps she took as she walked on the wire, extending her arms for balance while clutching a brightly colored balloon. She sang songs accompanied by a small chorus while she tiptoed across the wire. Con Colleano, attired in a bullfighter's costume, danced a few bolero steps as he traversed a slack wire. He was noted for the difficult front somersault which he accomplished on the wire. In another act which invariably mesmerized the audience Harold Alzana walked from the ground to the top of the tent on a wire strung at a forty-five degree angle.

In 1923 young Karl Wallenda, on the threshold of his career, walked across the Danube River on a cable. Subsequently he and his troupe distinguished themselves by carrying out with exquisite precision two of the most dangerous stunts on the high wire—inching across on bicycles and creating the three-level human pyramid. The epic "walk to fame" 750 feet above the Tallulah River in Georgia in 1970 celebrated Karl Wallenda's fiftieth year on the wire. It was also the longest and most daring solo act this agile performer had ever attempted. "You have to want to do it. . . .and you need energetic willpower," Wallenda revealed after the historic walk.

German-born Karl Wallenda came from a family of circus entertainers originally from Austria-Hungary. His great grandfather was the leader of a traveling troupe of jugglers and tumblers, his grandfather was an animal trainer and his grandmother was an

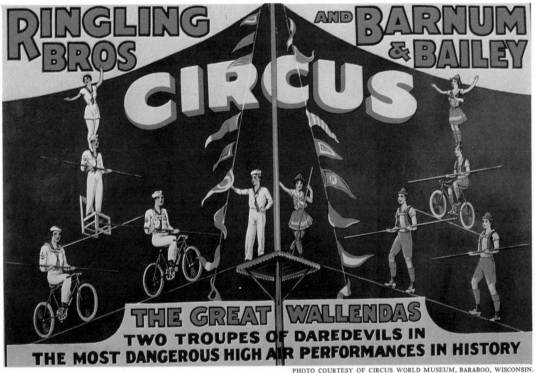

acrobat. His mother had been a trapeze artist in Germany before coming to this country. Today in his late sixties still handsome Karl Wallenda, master of the high wire, numbers seven generations of performers in his family. Two daughters, Carla and Jenny, have at one time or another been members of the family troupe. The performing Wallendas now include two grandchildren, Tina age twenty and Lila age eighteen. The other partner in the Wallenda quartet is Chilean Louis Murillo.

Wallenda began to show an interest in acrobatics and tumbling as a young boy growing up in Magdeburg, Germany. During World War I circus jobs were not readily available, and for a brief time he worked in a coal mine. When an ad appeared in the newspapers seeking a "handstander," Wallenda responded, never dreaming that the handstands were to be performed on the shoulders of a man forty feet above the ground! It was with the well-known German wire walker, Louis Weitzman, that sixteen-year-old Karl Wallenda began his career.

Young and full of ambition, Wallenda left the Weitzman act after a year to form his own group. With his brother Herman and two other acrobats, Karl Wallenda created the first high-wire tableau in which performers stood on each other's shoulders to form a human pyramid. The new troupe made its successful debut in Milan, Italy, in 1922. In 1927 when playing in Havana, Cuba, their act was seen by John Ringling, who was always scouting for fresh talent. He immediately signed the group for his circus. "The Flying Wallendas," as they were known in those days, came to the United States and opened in Madison Square

Top: Four of the Wallenda family perform headstands on high wire.

Center: Pyramid of four Wallendas crossing wire on bicycles, 1943.

Bottom: Seven members of the Wallenda troupe on the high wire moments before fall on January 30, 1962, when two members were killed.

ALL PHOTOS UNITED PRESS INTERNATIONAL

Garden a year later. At the end of their first appearance before an American audience the human pyramid drew an unprecedented fifteen-minute standing ovation. The Wallendas stayed with the Greatest Show on Earth from 1928 until 1946. Since then they have continued with their daring high-wire act at circus benefits and under other auspices.

Appearing with the Wallendas in the early days was a tiny, Munich-born acrobat, Helen, whom Karl Wallenda married in 1930. Helen Wallenda retired in 1959 after a thirty-two-year career on the high wire. When her daughter Carla was pregnant her mother Helen, a gallant trouper, returned to the act because they had a "contract to fulfill."

The Wallendas have been plagued by misfortune and tragedy during their many years on the high wire. The human pyramid act is generally performed forty feet above the ground without a net, sending shivers of apprehension through the crowds. Willy Wallenda, another of Karl's brothers, was killed in a fall in Sweden in 1933. When the back wheel of his bicycle came off the wire, he fell, landing in a net they happened to be using at the time. On the rebound he was thrown against a wall. He died of his injuries not long after. Since then, Karl has mistrusted safety nets, considering them more of a hazard than a help. "When a performer falls from the high wire into a net, his gear — poles, shoulder bars, bicycle or chair — usually falls upon him."

In Akron, Ohio, in 1934, Helen Wallenda, who was at the peak of the pyramid, fell when a guy rope became loose and the group lost their balance. Miraculously, she was saved by Karl, who grabbed the cable with his hands and then caught her with his legs as she fell past. He held her until some circus workers could safely catch her in a canvas blanket. The Wallendas then went hand over hand on the cable to safety.

Karl Wallenda, patriarch of the family of high-wire artists, crossing Tallulah Gorge in 1970.

The Wallendas were up on the high wire when the terrible circus tent fire occurred in Hartford, Connecticut, in 1944. When they heard the word "Fire!" and the band begin to play the disaster music, "Stars and Stripes Forever," they swiftly slid to the ground, but not before their costumes had been singed. A portion of burning canvas fell on Karl's wife, Helen, as she landed on the ground, but she was not seriously harmed. The troupe immediately joined in the rescue work helping to get the people out of the burning tent. The daring Wallenda family not only survived this catastrophe but also lived through the harrowing experience of being on the high wire when a major earthquake struck Nicaragua.

Death caught up again with the brave band of performers when the Wallendas were locked into their pyramid, well over thirty feet in the air. The Wallendas were appearing at a Shrine Circus at the Detroit Coliseum on January 30, 1962. Six thousand people had come to witness the most spectacular wire walking act in America. They were finishing the seven-man pyramid which they always saved for the finale. Four men were walking the cable, balancing two other men on poles connected to their shoulders. Seventeen-year-old Jana Schepp, a niece of Karl Wallenda, was perched on a chair at the top of the high structure. The four men on the first row were led by Dieter Schepp, Jana's brother. Both brother and sister had been brought here by Karl Wallenda from East Germany after World War II. Dieter's fingers began to lose their grasp on the balancing pole. He tried to raise it up slightly to regain his hold, which a solo performer is able to do readily, but his fingers could not stay around the pole. He screamed, "Ich kann nicht mehr halten!" (I can't hold any longer!) The pole slipped out of his hands, and he fell, pulling most of the group poised on the high wire down with him.

Karl Wallenda later stated that "The pole is our life. When you have it, then you can always recover your balance." Jana, at the top, was caught by Karl and a cousin, Gunther Wallenda. They dropped her into a net improvised by some circus people below, and the two Wallendas made their way hand over hand to the end of the wire. Of those who fell, Dieter Schepp and Richard Faughnan, Karl's son-in-law, were both crushed to death; Mario Wallenda, Karl's adopted son, was gravely injured and has been partially paralyzed ever since. Karl himself suffered a cracked pelvis and numerous other injuries. He was rushed to the hospital but insisted on returning to the act the following evening. Back on the wire, he could not force himself to look down. There remained the indelible picture of the boys, their balancing poles, the bars and the chair.

Since that horrible tragedy in 1962, the Wallendas have abandoned the seven-man pyramid and work as a group of four. They still continue to move dangerously across the wire in a three-deck pyramid with two men on the first row, one man standing on a bar connected to their shoulders and a girl sitting on a chair at the top. Tragedy has continued, however, to pursue the famous family. In 1963 "Miss Rietta," Helen Wallenda's sister, was killed in a fifty-foot fall from a wire in Omaha, Nebraska.

The Wallendas live in a neat, white frame house in Sarasota, Florida. In their backyard, Karl's grandchildren are hoisted onto their grandfather's shoulders, and he trains yet another generation to follow in his footsteps.

Karl Wallenda has considered retirement several times, but he claims he would rather "work, myself, than see others work." This incredible man, despite many tragedies and mishaps, expresses his greatest desire — to walk across the Grand Canyon, for to him, "To be on the wire is to live."

79

17
Parades and Wagons

Jubilee in the Streets

Swaying elephants, caged wild animals, glittering wagons and performers followed the crimson and gold bandwagon from which musicians blared out stirring marches and lively circus tunes. As the colorful line of heavy, horse-drawn wagons jolted past, with the shrill sounds of the calliope bringing up the rear, spectators often followed the parade to the circus lot and, the circus owners fervently hoped, to the ticket office. Such free and gaudy pageants promoting the circus are now only a glorious memory.

Elaborate street parades were an important feature of the circus in the years between 1880 and 1920. This was the ultimate advertisement and provided the townspeople with a taste of what the circus had to offer. Bills had been posted several days previously announcing the arrival of the show. But the gala promenade of performers and animals making their noisy and vivid entrance into town confirmed the arrival of the circus.

As early as Roman times, drivers in gilded chariots had paraded on their way to the gory spectacles at the Colosseum. In medieval times wandering minstrels danced and sang in the streets to attract an audience. During the Renaissance, decorated wagons rolled down cobbled streets in city festivals. Some were designed by famous painters, including Rubens.

Early in America's history, a cavorting clown riding a mule down a town road enticed people to come see a visiting circus troupe. Musicians riding in a cart were subsequently added, and the circus parade began to take form. After Seth B. Howes brought back painted, ornamental wagons from a European tour in the second half of the last century, American circus companies began to vie with one another in producing these flamboyant show vehicles.

Old-timers recall that a circus parade was "only as good as its wagons." The quantity and variety of elaborate parade vehicles was a yardstick to determine how good the show would be. The "Grand and Gorgeous Public Procession" of the Forepaugh Show in 1883 included "25 Monster Elephants, 40 Sunbright Chariots, Droves of Camels, and 300 Handsome Horses," an impressive assemblage.

Lumbering along near the end of most processions were the huge elephants caparisoned with spangled and bejeweled blankets.

Below left: Poster featuring Barnum & Bailey Continent parade wagons. They were built to commemorate the show's return from Europe in 1903.

Right: Sunburst wheels, on parade wagons created a kaleidoscopic effect.

Attendants in pith helmets sat on the heads of the pachyderms. Sometimes it was performers who were perched on top or were ensconced in howdahs. Coming up last was the powerful steam calliope whose ear-shattering music preceded its arrival. Despite the noise and the accompanying shower of coal particles from its stack, people followed the calliope in Pied Piper manner on its course back to the circus lot.

Perhaps the finest and the most extravagant parade in circus history was the one staged by the Barnum and Bailey Circus in 1903 in New York to celebrate the company's triumphant five-year tour of Europe. An outstanding feature of the moving festival was the record size Two Hemispheres bandwagon built at a cost of $40,000 by the Sebastian Wagon Works of New York.

The American circus wagons in essence were a vital folk art and are worthy of a closer look. The first ornamented wagons had biblical and landscape scenes painted on their sides. Later, richly carved bas-relief designs became characteristic. Their similarity to European religious sculpture is more than accidental for many of the wood-carvers had worked in the churches of Italy and Germany before coming to America.

The first bandwagon used by the Ringling Brothers was an old dray wagon with an eagle and a simulated mirror made of tin placed on either side. This wagon was constructed and carved by a cousin of the Ringlings, Henry Moeller, who later became well-known in the field.

During the forty years that the art of wood carving on wagons flourished, only a handful of companies existed whose skilled craftsmen did the intricate cutting and painting. Measurements and a general description of what the circus owners wanted were provided. After the panels were made they were shipped to the winter quarters of the circus. The

Bode Wagon Works of Cincinnati, the Sullivan and Eagles Company of Peru, Indiana, the Moeller Brothers of Baraboo, Wisconsin, the Fielding Brothers Company and Sebastian Wagon Works, both of New York, were notable among circus wagon builders. One circus company, the Gollmar Brothers Circus, not only constructed their own vehicles but did the wood carving on them as well.

There were two basic kinds of circus wagons: the parade wagons and the work wagons. Parade wagons included the bandwagon, the tableau wagons, the cage wagons and the calliope. The sturdy work wagons (called wagons whether they were motorized or horse-drawn) were unadorned and had a utilitarian purpose—to carry and transport heavy circus equipment such as canvas, ropes, stakes and other gear necessary for the tented city. Bandwagons were pressed into doing double duty since they were also used as baggage haulers during non-parade hours.

Parade wagons were constructed of seasoned oak, hard maple or hickory wood. Red was the dominant color used and the more elaborate carvings were gold-leafed. All of the wagons were numbered; many were also given names which not only matched their designs or themes but also indicated their purpose. Generally no two were alike and each was assigned a specific place in the line-up.

The multi-colored bandwagons were considered the "kings" in the wheeled caravan. Of those which have survived the passage of time, there are several which circus buffs and visitors to circus museums agree are outstanding examples of wagon artistry. Noteworthy among these is the Lion and Mirror bandwagon. This attractive white and gilded carriage with its massive carved figures and irregularly shaped mirrors was unique. Originally it was a "telescoping" tableau wagon —

81

Circus wagons below, from left to right:
Hagenback-Wallace cage wagon, France tableau
wagon (1919), Arthur Brothers wagon painted with
traditional tiger, Barnum Cinderella float (1880),
America calliope (orginally a tableau wagon, 1903),
Lion and Mirror bandwagon (1879).

that is, its platform could be raised and lowered by means of the windlass. On the platform were set life-size carvings of St. George and dragon. When the Ringlings acquired it from the Adam Forepaugh Circus in 1890, the allegorical figures were removed and seats added for musicians. It became their number one bandwagon and was used by their circus for twenty-eight years. Presently this masterpiece is displayed at the Circus World Museum in Baraboo, Wisconsin.

The Two Hemispheres bandwagon, which led the famous 1903 Barnum and Bailey parade, was ten and a half feet high, eight feet wide and its body was twenty-eight feet long. Though most bandwagons generally had the same carved bas-relief designs on both sides, the Two Hemispheres differed in that one side bore a wood-carved Eastern Hemisphere while the other carried the Western Hemisphere.

Another splendidly crafted bandwagon was the white and gold Swan bandwagon, built in 1907 by the Moellers and used by several companies including the Forepaugh-Sells, the Christy Brothers and the Ringling Brothers circuses.

The New York company of Fielding Brothers built the Five Graces bandwagon for the Adam Forepaugh Circus in 1878. There were only three graces in classical mythology, and circus historians believe that the central figure on the wagon panel is actually Columbia flanked by the four seasons. It was the most

widely traveled wagon of its kind; after being used in the parades of various other companies, Barnum and Bailey acquired it and it appeared in European tours from 1898 to 1902. Later, it went to the Ringling Brothers and Barnum & Bailey Combined Shows. A hitch of forty matched horses pulled the wagon.

The tableau wagon (shortened to tab wagon by circus people) were wood-carved floats which depicted continents, nations of the world and familiar characters from mythology, fairy tales or nursery rhymes. Performers dressed in glittering fairy-tale raiment in keeping with the tableau's theme often rode on top of the wagon. If the wagon's motif was taken from a foreign nation such as Russia or Arabia then the top riders dressed as Cossacks or Harem Girls, etc.

The Continent tableau wagons had designs which were inspired by the stone sculptures circus officials had seen at the Prince Albert Memorial in London. Wood carvings representing the different countries of each continent were placed across the upper part of the wagons. Painted bas-relief heads of the peoples of various nations appeared on the lower portion of each side. A large circular insignia with the name of the continent in wooden letters appeared in the center of the panel. Both the Asia and the America wagons were originally built at less than their present height. The America was later converted into a calliope.

Floats were miniature wagons which depicted various stories. Perhaps one of the most charming was the pony-drawn Cinderella float. This is one of seven scenes from fairy tales built in the 1880's for the Barnum and Bailey Circus. Its builder is unknown. The exquisitely rendered figures show a kneeling Prince placing a slipper on the beautiful chargirl's foot.

Cage wagons holding pacing jungle cats, polar bears, hyenas and other animals were also in the parade line-up. They were included to lure the spectators to the show. Displayed in cleverly designed turnabout cages was a menagerie collection of exotic birds.

The calliope, a monstrous vehicle producing earsplitting sounds, came after the other wagons had passed. Pronounced "cally-ope" by circus people, the name is a satirical one based on two Greek roots meaning beautiful-voiced. Joshua C. Stoddard is given credit for its popular use, though it is believed that his patent awarded in 1885 for "the new musical instrument to be played by the agency of steam or highly compressed air" was actually an improvement on an already existing idea. Calliope-like instruments had been used by the railroads during the Civil War to play patriotic tunes.

The sound of the calliope was produced when a player pressed the keys of the instrument, in turn opening the whistle valves and allowing steam to blow through them. These steam whistles had a range of several octaves.

A boiler, located at the rear of the calliope wagon, produced the steam. At times the steam pressure varied. As a result, the raucous sounds were even more discordant because they tended to be out of tune.

By the 1920's the ostentatious rolling pageants became impractical. People felt that once they had seen the parade it was hardly worth the price of admission to attend the actual show. More automobiles on the streets and, most significant, the increased economic burden of circuses made the parades an unnecessary extravagance. The bigger resplendent street marches ground to a halt around 1920. The gingerbread-fancy wagons were no longer produced. In the smaller circuses the last regular street parade was held in 1939. The hundred or so elegant vehicles which remain may be seen at the circus museums in Sarasota, Florida, and Baraboo, Wisconsin.

Nostalgia has prompted several circus companies to attempt to revive this great tradition, and occasional street marches on a lesser scale have been staged. None of these have become permanent realities.

On the Fourth of July the people of Milwaukee line the streets each year to watch a street parade abounding in all of its former color and glitter. The authentic wagons in the parade are sponsored by one of the local brewing companies. It is apparent to all who attend this gala event that the magnificent sights and sounds of a bygone era have lost none of their fascination.

18
The Circus Today

The Magic Continues

Troupers with the Ringling Bros. and Barnum & Bailey Circus wept when the momentous announcement was made on the circus grounds in Pittsburgh in July 1956 that the days of its tented circus were over. Faced with mounting costs and the hazards of battling the weather to put on a tented show, John Ringling North decided to call it quits and ordered the circus back to winter quarters with the season only half over. But The Greatest Show on Earth certainly was not dead. The next year it was back, playing the larger cities by booking in buildings which were better lighted, more comfortable and adjacent to paved parking lots. It was soon apparent that the change from tent to amphitheaters was not only necessary but wise. Although some smaller circus companies continued to perform under canvas, a new era had begun.

Sideshows and the menagerie were eliminated in the new Ringling Brothers show. But clowns, lovely ladies, daring trapeze artists, somersaulting acrobats on the high wire, fearsome wild animal acts and loping elephants have all remained. The smells of popcorn, peanuts and hot dogs are still there and in its present enclosed atmosphere the circus has lost none of its tanbark appeal.

The American circus has come a long way from the early equestrian shows which President George Washington attended. With the indomitable spirit which has characterized it down through the years, the circus has survived wars, depressions and tragic fires. This amazing institution has endured despite the competition of an increasing number of leisure time activities. The circus continues to lure millions of dedicated fans — witness the crowds at any circus today.

Many aspects of the circus have changed. The mode of travel of the major circuses has evolved from early mud wagon days, progressing to railroads, then to the use of motor trucks. The circuses of the 1970's are transported almost entirely in capacious vans. Housing for personnel which at various times consisted of wagons, tents and railroad car berths is now provided by mobile homes and hotel rooms; and the familiar landmark of the circus backyard, the wash-water bucket, is no longer in sight. Gone also are the problems and expense of preparing and serving employees three meals daily in a cookhouse tent.

Considering the transformations which have taken place in our culture, it is remarkable that the American circus has survived at all. After enjoying tremendous popularity in its golden years from the turn of the century to the early twenties, the circus entered a long period of decline. With great resilience it has since recovered its vigor and picked itself up by its spangled bootstraps.

Over the years circus company mergers and assimilations have been a common fact of circus life. The biggest news of the circus world in the late 1960's was the sale of the Ringling Circus to Irvin and Israel Feld and Judge Roy Hofheinz after nearly a decade of negotiations. The price is said to have been in the neighborhood of eight million dollars.

When Irvin Feld, an inventive and astute businessman took over, he introduced numerous innovations which have made the circus more viable. With flare, imagination and showmanship, he has managed to maintain the show's prestigious reputation. He established two separate units under the Ringling banner in 1969. The Red unit and the Blue unit crisscross the continent, each following a different route. On alternate years they exchange routes. The public therefore views a different show each season, and the performers are assured of a two-year contract. The 600 people in the two units will visit ninety-one cities in the United States and Canada in the current year.

Ringling Bros. and Barnum & Bailey Circus
continues to offer its special brand
of entertainment. The circus has turned
full circle and now performs mostly in closed
amphitheatres from which it sprang.

PHOTO COURTESY OF RINGLING BROS.–BARNUM & BAILEY COMBINED SHOWS, INC.

Irvin Feld scouts all over Europe for new acts, and each edition of this circus, now in its 102nd year, continues to outdazzle the previous three-ring extravaganza. Currently the amazing high-wire duo of Mendez and Seitz draws gasps of apprehension and admiration as one somersaults over the head of his partner. The band accompanies their fast-paced act with lively Latin music. The King Charles Troupe, a group of black unicycle-riding basketball players, weaves a combination of comedy and athletic skills. Before the eyes of a speechless audience, Pablo Noel, a wild animal trainer from the Feija-Castilla Circus in Spain, brusquely parts the jaws of a fierce-looking lion and inserts his head for a few moments.

Perhaps the most outstanding attraction, reserved for the end of the show, is the "Flying Gaonas." Their difficult mid-air ma-neuvers, including triple somersaults and two-and-a-half turn pirouettes, are performed with enormous style and ease. They appear to have the charismatic quality which makes true circus heroes and heroines. The Big One includes many more such stellar acts like those of Gunther Gebel-Williams and Charley Baumann, but the producer, Mr. Irvin Feld, considers his *entire* show to be the star.

The Mattel Corporation, which purchased the Ringling Brothers and Barnum & Bailey Circus in 1970, has made no change in command. Mr. Irvin Feld has continued to serve as president of the circus, which is operated as a wholly-owned subsidiary of the parent company, and both have benefited by the merger.

While the Ringling show has seen a consistently rising attendance in the past few

UNITED PRESS INTERNATIONAL

Left: Modern circus wagon, a low-slung aluminum car, slips easily into tunnel car of circus train.

Below left: Charley Baumann and "friend." New names are always being added to the roster of circus heroes and heroines.

years, smaller companies have shown gains as well. These circus organizations include some venerable titles: Hamid-Morton, King Brothers, Sells and Gray, James Brothers, Pollack Brothers, Hunt Brothers, Carson & Barnes and the Hubert Castle circuses among others. Also, many individual acts are being booked for specialized shows such as television and nightclub performances. The indoor circuses, presently about forty in number, are generally better attended than the outdoor, tented shows. Many circus companies today perform for the benefit of hospitals, fraternal or other charitable organizations.

Each spring about fifteen smaller old-time circuses continue to take to the road. The Hoxie Brothers Circus, one of the largest of such tented shows, travels from Florida to Michigan for a twenty-nine-week season. The magical feat of erecting a canvas tent is accomplished at each stay of their tour.

BROWN BROTHERS

Eight big elephants help in the rigging and hoisting of the Big Top. The huge sections of the tent are laced together by the show's roustabouts with the aid of local "towners."

The purple trucks of the Hoxie Circus filled with all of their gear travel to Army bases, hospitals and available lots in thirteen different states. Like other traveling shows, this circus still maintains a sideshow featuring a fire-eater, sword swallower and a snake dancer who performs with a boa constrictor.

When asked why they continue day after day with their rigorous schedule of nearly 200 one-night stands, a seasoned trouper explained that one simply has to love this sort of life. The camaraderie among the performers in the smaller circus is perhaps one of its strongest assets. There are some who feel that this closeness has been lost in large circus organizations.

In virtually all of the circuses today there is a heavy emphasis on overseas talent — the roll call sounds like a veritable United Nations. Although suitable American talent is constantly sought, circus agents still import many European acts, thereby providing a rich international mosaic. As the ringmaster of the Hoxie Brothers Circus said in a recent magazine interview ". . . all nationalities; all languages. Too bad the rest of the world can't get along like we do."*

Some of today's stars are second and third generation artists of the same family. The Hanneford Circus, another of the smaller three-ring circuses, has its origins in the early 1800's. A young Irishman, Michael Hanneford, toured the countryside of England with Wombwell's Menagerie. The family has carried on with the circus tradition ever since that time.

The Hannefords came to America in 1915 as part of the Ringling Brothers Circus. This

*John Fetterman, "On the Road With An Old-Time Circus."

Two complete units operate under
the Ringling banner. The Red and the
Blue units crisscross the continent, each
following a different route.

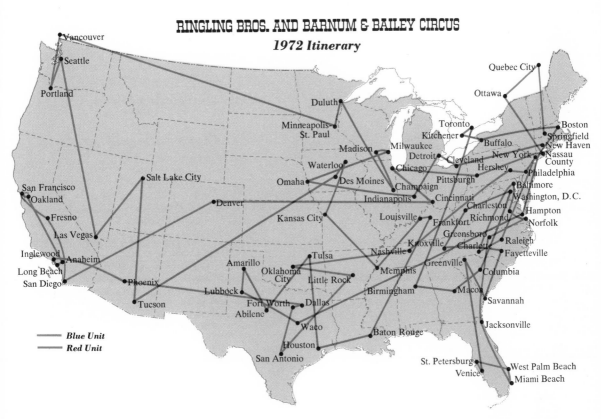

RINGLING BROS. AND BARNUM & BAILEY CIRCUS
1972 Itinerary

Blue Unit
Red Unit

association lasted for fifty years, but they are now appearing under their own aegis. This well-known band of troupers included "Poodles" Hanneford, the celebrated riding clown. The present generation is headed by Tommy Hanneford, who appears in the equestrian act and other portions of the program. A rather unusual display in the current production of this circus features ferocious leopards and pumas in the steel-caged arena. They are put through their paces by their trainer—an exotic female!

When the old-time circus advance man put up posters on the barns and fences of hamlets and towns, the proclamation meant that a little excitement was going to come into otherwise routine lives. The entire family eagerly awaited the excursion to the show

grounds. The circus today, either large or small version, is still very much "alive and kicking" and still delivering that special form of entertainment. The future bodes well for the circus as long as there are eager children, and parents with memories.

In an article entitled "The Circus" in the Ringling Brothers Circus program of 1953, the late Ernest Hemingway eloquently expressed his feelings on the subject:

The circus is the only ageless delight you can buy for money . . . It is the only spectacle I know that while you watch it, gives the quality of a truly happy dream.

Or as the poet, e.e. cummings, more succinctly put it:

Damn everything but the circus.

Glossary—Circus Lingo

There is a particular jargon that belongs exclusively to the world of the circus. As in any close group, circus lingo evolved from convenience and daily usage. A few expressions were abridged from longer words but carry some of their original flavor; others were coined or invented as the need arose. A number were derived from the Italian and French languages; still others were contributions from the Romany tongue of the gypsies. Gradually all of these words became threads woven into the rich tapestry of the circus.

The following glossary is a compilation of some of the more common terms, including those which have become outdated as the circus changed.

Aba-daba — Any dessert that was served in the cookhouse.

Advance Men — Men who go into towns ahead of the circus to put up heralds and posters publicizing the arrival of the circus.

Alfalfa — Paper money.

All Out and Over — Entire performance is concluded.

Annie Oakley — A complimentary ticket or free pass.

Auguste Clown — A clumsy, slapstick clown who wears no traditional costume.

Back Door — Performer's entrance to the Big Top.

Bally — A platform used by spielers to give the crowd an idea of the show to be seen inside.

Ballyhoo — The spiel shouted in front of the side-show to attract attention.

Banner — The canvas paintings in front of the side-show depicting the attractions within.

Bibles — Programs or souvenir magazines.

Big Bertha or The Big One — Ringling Brothers and Barnum & Bailey Circus.

Big Top — The main tent used for the performance.

Blowdown — When the tents are blown down by a storm.

Blow Off — The end of the show when the concessionaires come out.

Blues — The general admission seats.

Boss Canvas Man — The man whose job is to decide exactly where and how the tents should be put up at a new circus lot.

Boss Hostler — The man who traveled ahead of the mud shows to mark the way for the caravan; sometimes used to denote the one in charge of all horses in a show.

Bulls — Elephants (whether male or female).

Bunce — Profits.

Butcher — Refreshment merchants; peddler of lemonade, candy, pretzels and other edibles.

Calliope — A musical instrument consisting of a series of steam whistles played like an organ; pronounced *cally-ope* by circus people.

Carpet Clown — A clown who works either among the audience or on arena floor.

Catcher — A member of a trapeze act who catches the flyer after he has released himself from the bar in a flying return act.

Cats — Lions, tigers, leopards, panthers.

Cattle Guard — A set of low seats placed in front of the general admission seats to accommodate overflow audiences.

Center Pole or King Pole — The first pole of the tent to be raised. It is about 60 feet high, weighs about a ton and holds the peak of the tent.

Character Clown — A clown who usually dresses in a tramp costume.

Charivari — A noisy whirlwind entrance of clowns; also called shivaree or chivaree.

Cherry Pie — Extra work done by circus personnel for extra pay.

Clem — A fight.

Clown Alley — A section of tent where clowns put on their makeup and store their props.

Clown Stop — A brief appearance of the clowns while the props are being changed.

Clown Walk-Around — A parade of clowns during which time they may stop and do their acts.

Come-In — The period when the public is entering the arena before the circus performance begins.

Dog and Pony Show — A derisive term for a small circus.

Dona — A woman.

Donikers — Restrooms.

Doors! — Call meaning to let the public in.

Dressage — The art of showing trained horses; animal paces are guided by subtle movements of rider's body.

Dressed — When tickets are distributed so that all sections are filled with no obviously empty areas.

Ducat Grabber — Door tender or ticket collector.

Dukey or Duckie — Box lunch. The first cookhouse was known as "Hotel du Quai." When pronounced quickly it sounded like "dukey" and the name stuck.

Dukey Run — Any circus run longer than an overnight haul.

En Férocité — The term used by European circuses to describe American wild animal acts, as opposed to their "tableau" presentations.

Equestrian Director — Ringmaster (derived from early circuses featuring primarily equestrian performers).

Feet Jump — In equestrian riding — standing with the feet together, bareback rider jumps from the ground or teeterboard on to back of a running horse.

Fink or Larry — A broken novelty such as a torn balloon.

First of May — A novice performer in his first season on a circus show.

Flatties — People.

Flip-Flaps — The trick of flipping from a standing position to the hands while bareback rider is on a running horse.

Flyers — Aerialists, especially those in flying return acts.

Flying Squadron — The first section of a circus to reach the lot.

Framing a Show — Planning a circus production.

Funambulist — Rope walker. From Latin: *funis*-rope, and *ambulare*- to walk.

Funny Ropes — Extra ropes added to regular ones, usually at angles, to give extra stability and spread to canvas tent.

Gaffer — Circus manager.

Galop — Fast tempo band melodies used in certain exits and entrances.

Gilly — Anyone not connected with the circus; an outsider. See also Towner.

Gilly Wagon — Extra small wagon or cart used to carry light pieces of equipment around the lot.

Graft — A piece of work — sometimes easy, sometimes hard.

Grafters — Gamblers who often trail a show.

Grotesque — Type of clown who wears exaggerated costume and carries outlandish props.

Guys — Heavy ropes or cables that help to support poles or high wire rigging.

Harlequin — A clown of the commedia dell'arte who dressed in a diamond-patterned costume and who wore a black mask.

Heralds — Circus advertisements, approximately 9 x 20 inches, which can be pasted down or handed out. They are not in color and consist of type and pictures.

Hey Rube! — Traditional battle cry of circus people in fights with townspeople.

High School Horse — A horse who has been taught fancy steps in special riding academies. See also Dressage.

Hits — Places such as walls of grain elevators, barns, buildings, or fences on which heralds and posters were pasted.

Home Run — The trip from Home Sweet Home back to winter quarters.

Home Sweet Home — The last stand of the season when bill posters usually pasted one pack of posters upside down.

Homy — A man. A bona homy is a good man.

Horse — One thousand dollars.

Horse Feed — Poor returns from poor business.

Horse Opery — Any circus (jokingly).

Howdah or Howdy — A seat, often with a canopy, on the back of an elephant or camel.

Human Oddities — Sideshow of abnormal persons.

Iron-Jaw Trick — An aerial stunt using a metal bit and apparatus which fits into the performer's mouth. Thus suspended he performs his tricks.

Jackpots — Tall tales about the circus.

Jill — A girl.

Joey — A clown (derived from Joseph Grimaldi, a famous clown in England of the 18th century).

Jonah's Luck — Unusually bad weather or mud.

Jump — The distance between performances in different towns.

Jump Stand — An additional booth near the front door used to sell extra tickets during a rush by spectators.

Kicking Sawdust — Following the circus or being a part of it.

Kid Show — A sideshow.

Kiester — Wardrobe trunk.

Kinker — Any circus performer (originally only an acrobat).

Layout Man — The lot superintendent who decides the location of various tents.

Lead Stock — Any haltered animals other than horses; e.g., camels, llamas, zebras and others.

Liberty Acts or Liberty Horses — Horses trained to work "free" in the ring without any riders.

Lift — The natural bounce which lifts bareback rider from ground to back of a running horse.

Little People — Midgets or dwarfs.

Lot — Land leased by the circus for performances.

Lot Lice — Local townspeople who arrive early to watch unloading of the circus and stay late.

Main Guy — Guy rope to hold up center pole in the Big Top.

March, The — The street parade.

Mechanic — The leather safety harness which is worn by flyers in practice sessions and controlled by man below.

Midway — The area near the main entrance where the sideshows are located and concessionaires sell refreshments and souvenirs.

Mud Show — Circus show that traveled overland, not on rails. So named because the wagon wheels were frequently mired in mud.

Nanty — Nothing.

On the Show — Performers and all others connected to the circus. The term "with" the show is not used.

Opposition Paper — Advertising posters which were put up by competing circuses.

Pad Room — Dressing Room. So called because riders hang their pads there.

Paper — Circus posters.

Parlari — Circus people talking.

Perch Act — A balancing act involving use of apparatus upon which one person is performing while being balanced by another.

Picture Gallery — A tattooed man.

Pie-Car — The dining car of a railroad train.

Pitchmen — The salesmen at concessions on the midway.

Planges — Aerialist's body swing-overs in which one hand and wrist are placed in padded rope loop.

Ponger — An acrobat.

Possom Belly — Extra storage box attached underneath a work wagon or railway car.

Quarter Poles — Poles which help support the weight of the canvas and take up the slack between center and side poles.

Rat Sheets — Advance posters or handbills with negative slant toward opposition.

Razorbacks — The men who load and unload railroad cars.

Read the Lot — Looking for tent stakes and other paraphernalia after the show is over and struck.

Red Wagon — Box office wagon, main office of circus; also money wagon. This was usually painted red though it could be any color.

Rig — To put up aerial rigging.

Rigging — The apparatus used in high wire or aerial acts.

Ring Banks or Curbs — Wooden curbing around the ring.

Ring Barn — Regulation-sized circus ring for practice at winter quarters.

Ring Horse — A horse which performs in the center ring. He is trained to maintain timing despite distractions.

Ring Stock — Circus animals which perform in the show, including horses, llamas, camels and ponies.

Risley Act — Three acrobats lying on their backs who toss a fourth acrobat from one to the other.

Roll-Ups — same as aerial planges.

Roman Riding — A rider standing on the backs of two horses.

Roper — A cowboy.

Rosinback — Horse used for bareback riding. So named because horses' backs were sprinkled with rosin to prevent rider from slipping.

Roustabout — A circus workman, laborer.

Rubbermen — The men who sell balloons.

Safety Loop — The loop part of a web rope into which a performer places her wrist in aerial ballet numbers.

Segue — Music bridge used in changing from one tune to another without stopping.

Shanty or Chandelier — The man who works the lights.

Shill — A man used as a decoy; an employee who stands in line to make the box office look busy and walks in without paying.

Sky Boards — The decorated boards along top of cage wagons used in parades.

Slanger — Trainer of cats.

Sledge Gang — Crew of men who pounded in tent stakes.

Soft Lot — A wet or muddy lot.

Spec — Short form for spectacle. A colorful pageant which is a featured part of the show; formerly used as the opening number, now presented just before intermission.

Spec Girls — Comely show girls who appear in the grand spectacle.

Spieler — An announcer.

Splash Boards — Decorated bottom edge of cage wagons used in parades.

Stand — Any town where the circus plays.

Star Backs — More expensive reserved seats.

St. Louis — Doubles or seconds of food. So named because St. Louis engagement was played in two sections.

Strawhouse — A sell-out house. Straw was spread on ground for spectators to sit upon in front of general admission seats.

Swags — Prizes.

Tableau Wagons — Ornamental parade wagons. Costumed circus performers rode atop them.

Tail Up — Command to an elephant to follow in line.

Talkers — Ticket takers for sideshow; never called "barkers."

Tanbark — The shredded bark from trees from which tannin has been extracted and used to cover circus arena ground.

The Big One — Ringling Brothers and Barnum & Bailey Circus.

Toot Up — To get attention of spectators by playing the calliope.

Tops — Tents; for example, dressing tops are where the performers dress for show.

Towners — Townspeople; any outsiders. See also Gilly.

Troupers — Circus entertainers.

Trunk Up — Command to an elephant to raise his trunk in a salute.

Turnaway — A sold-out show.

Twenty-four-hour Man — An advance man who works one day ahead of circus.

Wait Brothers Show — Ringling Brothers and Barnum & Bailey Show. So called because the posters read, "Wait for the Big Show."

Web — Dangling canvas-covered rope suspended from swivels from the top of the tent.

Web Girl — Female who performs on web in aerial ballet sequence.

Web Sitter — Ground man who holds or controls the web for aerialists.

Windjammer — A member of a circus band.

With It — An expression meaning loyalty to the show.

Zanies — Clowns.

Bibliography

American Heritage, *Great Days of the Circus.* American Heritage Publishing Co., New York, 1962.

Bailey, Olga, *Mollie Bailey, The Circus Queen of the Southwest.* Thomas Publishing Co., Harben Spotts Co., Dallas, 1943.

Ballantine, Bill, HOLIDAY, *Stupendous! Titanic! Colossal! Magnificent!* April, 1970. Vol. 47, No. 4.

Ballantine, Bill, *Wild Tigers and Tame Fleas.* Rinehart & Company, New York, 1958.

Beatty, Clyde, *The Big Cage.* The Century Co., New York, 1933.

Brown, Maria Ward, *The Life of Dan Rice.* J. J. Little & Co., New York, 1901. (as quoted in Fenner and Fenner, *The Circus; Lure and Legend.* Prentice-Hall, Inc., Englewood Cliffs, N. J., 1970.)

Chindahl, George L., *A History of the Circus in America.* The Caxton Printers, Ltd., Caldwell, Idaho, 1959.

Cody, William F., *An Autobiography of Buffalo Bill.* Cosmopolitan Book Corporation, New York, 1920.

Country Beautiful Magazine Editors, *Circus!* Country Beautiful Foundation, Inc., Elm Grove, Wisconsin; Hawthorn Books, Inc., New York, 1964.

Durant, John and Alice, *Pictorial History of the American Circus.* A. S. Barnes and Co., Inc., Cranbury, New Jersey, 1957.

Fenner, Mildred Sandison and Fenner, Wolcott, *The Circus; Lure and Legend.* Prentice-Hall, Inc., Englewood Cliffs, New Jersey, 1970.

Fetterman, John, NATIONAL GEOGRAPHIC, *On the Road with an Old-Time Circus.* March, 1972, Vol. 141, No. 3.

Fox, Charles Philip, *A Ticket to the Circus.* Superior Publishing Co., Bramhall House, New York, 1959.

Fox, Charles Philip, *The Circus Comes To Town.* Inland Press, Milwaukee, 1963.

Fox, Charles Philip and Parkinson, Tom, *The Circus in America.* Country Beautiful Foundation, Inc., Waukesha, Wisconsin, 1969.

Garst, Shannon, *Annie Oakley.* Julian Messner, Inc., New York, 1958.

Hamid, George A., *Circus, as told to his Son.* Sterling Publishing Co., Inc., New York, 1950.

Hunt, Charles T., *The Story of Mr. Circus.* The Record Press, Rochester, New Hampshire, 1954.

Hunter, J. Marvin, Sr., FRONTIER TIMES, *Mollie Bailey, The Great Showwoman.* April, 1950, Vol. 27, No. 7.

Johnson, Lillian, *Sarasota Herald Tribune,* "Making People Laugh is Gift of God." January 2, 1971.

Kelly, Emmett, with Kelley, F. Beverly, *Clown.* Prentice-Hall, Inc., New York, 1954.

Kunzog, John C., *The One Horse Show; The Life and Times of Dan Rice.* John C. Kunzog, Jamestown, New York, 1962.

Leonard, Elizabeth Jane and Goodman, Julia Cody, *Buffalo Bill; King of the Old West.* Library Publishers, New York, 1955.

LIFE, *Will They Make It?* (articles on the Wallendas), February 9, 1962, Vol. 52, No. 6.

LIFE, *The Funniest College on Earth.* Jan. 1, 1970, Vol. 68, No. 6.

LIFE, *Wallenda is at it Again.* July 31, 1970, Vol. 69, No. 5.

May, Earl Chapin, *The Circus From Rome to Ringling.* Dover Publications, New York, 1963.

M.D. (Medical News Magazine), *Prince of Humbug.* February, 1960, Vol. 4, No. 2.

Murray, Marian, *Circus! From Rome to Ringling.* Appleton-Century-Crofts, Inc., New York, 1956.

Newton, Douglas, *Clowns.* George G. Harrap & Co., Ltd., London, 1958.

North, Henry Ringling and Hatch, Alden, *The Circus Kings.* Doubleday & Co., Inc., Garden City, N. Y., 1960.

Papp, John and Craig, J. Marvyn, *Those Golden Years; The Circus.* John Papp, Schenectady, 1971.

Richardson, Vivian, *Dallas Morning News,* "Courage and Canvas." (article on Mollie Bailey), June 1, 1930.

Robbins, Peggy, AMERICAN LEGION, *The Life of Phineas T. Barnum.* September, 1971, Vol. 91, No. 3.

Rothe, Aline, *Houston Chronicle,* "Here Comes Mollie Bailey; Circus Queen of Texas." November 28, 1954.

Scharf, J. Thomas and Westcott, Thompson, *History of Philadelphia,* 1609-1884, Vol. 11, L. H. Everts Co., Philadelphia, 1884.

Sherwood, Robert Edmund, *Here We Are Again.* The Bobbs-Merrill Co., Indianapolis, 1926.

Taylor, Robert Lewis, *Center Ring; The People of the Circus.* Doubleday & Co., Inc., Garden City, N. Y., 1956.

Wallace, Irving, *The Fabulous Showman; The Life and Times of P. T. Barnum.* Alfred A. Knopf, New York, 1959.

Walsh, Richard J. in collaboration with Milton S. Salsbury, *The Making of Buffalo Bill.* The Bobbs-Merrill Co., Indianapolis, 1928.

Wardlow, Jean, *The Miami Herald,* "Weary Willie Misses the Fun." April 18, 1971.

Index